TIGER BOOKS INTERNATIONAL

POSITIS SIGNIS ET ANA
GLYPHIS TA IUSSU CLEME XIII PONT MAX OPUS
NI CVLTVAE

past and present

ROME

Text
Beppe Ceccato

Editing Supervision
Laura Accomazzo

Art Director
Patrizia Balocco Lovisetti

Graphic design
Anna Galliani

Translation
Ann Ghiringhelli
C.T.M.

To my parents, Giacomo and Carla, incurably curious and dedicated tourists in Rome.

1 A horse-drawn carriage in front of the Colosseum offers a typical picture-postcard scene of Rome, although fewer and fewer people now opt for this form of transport when touring the city centre.

2 The gifted work of Antonio Canova can be clearly seen in this sculpture of Paolina Borghese.

7 In this photograph we can see the famous statues of the Trevi Fountain.

This edition published in 1998 by TIGER BOOKS INTERNATIONAL PLC , 26a York Street Twickenham TW1 3LJ, England.

First published by Edizioni White Star. Title of the original edition: Roma.

ISBN 1-84056-021-5

Printed in Italy by Grafedit, Bergamo (Italy).
Colour separations by Fotomec, Turin (Italy).

CONTENTS

3-6 The Trevi Fountain is definitely the best-loved, most famous and most frequently described, photographed and filmed fountain in Rome. It is situated just a short way from the Quirinal and Palazzo Colonna, home of an important art gallery. Work on the fountain, commissioned by Pope Clement XII, was started in 1732 by Nicola Salvi and continued by Giuseppe Pannini eleven years later. It was eventually inaugurated by Pope Clement XIII in 1762. The monument, at the side of Palazzo Poli, is a glorious fusion of classical rigour and Baroque fantasy. A glance at this picture reveals all. Perfectly linear Corinthian columns support an upper storey with a balustrade topped by Clement XII's coat-of-arms. In distinct contrast are the graceful, allegorical figures "flowing" towards the ocean: a majestic Neptune on a shell-shaped chariot drawn by sea-horses.

SOLVTVM A·DOM·MDCCLXII

INTRODUCTION

8 top At the top of the staircase Castor and Pollux, with their horses, preside over the Capitol, the political hub of Rome for thousands of years. Datable to the late imperial period, these statues came from the Monte Cenci area, where there was a temple dedicated to the two gods. They were installed here in 1585, several years after Piazza del Campidoglio was re-designed by Michelangelo (succeeded by the architect Giacomo della Porta, who completed the project).

8 bottom This statue of Emperor Octavian Augustus, known as the "Augusto di Prima Porta", was discovered in the villa "ad Gallinas Albas" in 1863. It is now conserved in the new wing of the Museo Chiaromonti, part of the Vatican collections.

To write about Rome is no small undertaking. And an even greater challenge faces anyone attempting to interpret and judge the life of this age-old city, protagonist or at least runner-up of every epoch and situation, in good times and bad. Anything and everything can be said of Rome. That it is a stunning city goes without saying: its monuments and works of art - a magnet for tourists and scholars from every corner of the globe - speak for themselves. Think of the Imperial Fora, for instance, where excavations continue in the hope of unearthing further splendid traces of a bold and determined civilization, the creator - in the space of a few hundred years - of the world's most powerful empire; or the palaces of the Renaissance period when papal families spent fortunes embellishing dwellings and churches, almost competing to outshine one another for magnificence and patronage. It is self-evidently also an amusing and hospitable city. The easy-going, quick-witted Romans are themselves living proof of this, and there has to be a good reason why, if you ask visiting foreigners in which Italian city they'd like to live, the majority say 'Rome', without hesitating.
Even John Fante, an Italo-American writer - Bukowski's idol - known for his pungent remarks and disdain for romanticism, speaks nostalgically about Rome in his books and hopes to spend the last years of his life on

8-9 The Palatine Hill is a good vantage point from which to admire the Imperial Fora. Prominent amongst the ruins are the imposing remains of the Basilica of Maxentius, one of the largest buildings ever erected in ancient Rome (completed by Constantine and restructured at the end of the 4th century), and the church of Santa Francesca Romana.

9 top Trajan's Column is one of the few monuments of ancient Rome to have reached the Third Millennium intact. Formed of 25 blocks of marble, 350 cm across, it is entirely covered with bas-reliefs carved on a 10 mm base by an anonymous sculptor. The detailed scenes relate the emperor's heroic exploits during the Dacian wars.

Piazza Navona. Rome is all this, and much much more. Just think, for instance, of its 1,500 or more fountains. In the recent past these splendid creations, often commissioned by art-loving, power-thirsty popes, have inspired countless films and novels. Trevi, Piazza Navona, the Spanish Steps and Fontana Barcaccia: the city's most famous fountains evoke fleeting memories of bygone days and still vivid episodes that were emblematic of Italy from the Sixties onwards. Rome is a city of a thousand faces where each and every street and piazza lends itself to diverse interpretations. And no-one could be more aware of this than the great film directors and actors - foreigners as well as Italians - who turned countless tales of Rome into truly memorable films: Vittorio De Sica's Rome, brought to her knees and deprived of all hope by an endless war, as captured by the extraordinary expressiveness of Anna Magnani; the Rome of Federico Fellini, Rimini-born but Roman by adoption, who gave a face to human frailty, joy and despair in a postwar Italy in search of economic stability and innocent (and less innocent) pleasures; the Rome of Alberto Sordi, chaotic but resourceful; the Rome of Carlo Verdoni, as seen in his irresistible portrayals of "ordinary" Romans; the very different picture painted by Pier Paolo Pasolini, film director and poet, who laid bare a problem city with sprawling suburbs and streetwise youngsters ready to experience all that life can offer, including violence. As though cast as protagonist in one of his own tales, Pasolini was eventually the victim of the very violence he had exposed, generated by poverty and degradation. And there is also the Rome of Nanni Moretti, director and actor. In *Dear Diary* he trod forbidden ground with scenes set in the Fascist district of Garbatella with its ugly, box-like buildings. But as he roamed the streets on his inseparable Vespa, he managed to find something positive even in this not-so-pretty corner of the capital.

The message is clear: Rome is still Rome, from whatever viewpoint it is presented. It is Italy's capital irrespective of its denigrators, and Rome, city of art, is far different from the political Rome with which it is all too often associated. Admittedly this queen of cities has been sorely tried by irresponsible government, time and time again. In recent years however the people of Rome have voiced their desire for change and new lifeblood has been coursing through the city's veins. After almost thirty-five years, for example, there is again talk of a town planning scheme. This time the project for urban renewal does not set out to fill more spaces with bricks and concrete, it instead focuses on reorganizing public parks and gardens and tackling the blighted suburbs that encompass the city. In the last few years seventeen new green areas have

10-11 and 11 top Piazza Navona owes much of its fame to its three fountains. The Fontana di Nettuno, at the north end of the square, was designed by Giacomo della Porta and is similar in structure to the Fontana del Moro (by Bernini). For 300 years, until 1873, the fountain remained unadorned. Rome's city council then decided it should be completed and organized a design competition. The sole mandatory specification was that Bernini's style be maintained. The winner was the sculptor Antonio Della Bitta, who carved the figure of Neptune; the putti, sea nymphs, sea-horses and mascarons were created by Gregorio Zappalà.

12 top Over its long existence Castel Sant'Angelo has had many roles: imperial mausoleum, medieval citadel, symbol of papal power and now museum. Hadrian wanted a suitably grandiose resting-place for himself and his descendants and so broke with the tradition of burying Roman emperors in the Mausoleum of Augustus. The fortress, configured as a cylindrical structure resting on a square base, is believed to have been designed by Hadrian himself. Work on its construction began in A.D. 130 and was completed ten years later by Antoninus Pius.

12 bottom This photo highlights the delicately carved forms of the "angel with the lance", one of the statues on the Ponte Sant'Angelo.

13 Michelangelo's Pietà, *one of the world's most famous works of art, is displayed in a chapel in St.Peter's. Commissioned by Cardinal Jean de Bilheres de Lagraulas, Charles V's ambassador to Pope Alexander VI, it was created in 1498-99.*

14-15 The Flavian Amphitheatre - known to one and all as the Colosseum - stands 52 metres high and occupies an area of 3,357 sq.metres. It had an estimated capacity of 70,000 spectators. Extensively damaged through the passing centuries by fires and earthquakes, the amphitheatre was first converted into dwellings and eventually, in 1100s, into a fortress occupied by the Frangipane family. Around this time its marble and stone began to be removed and used to build new palaces and churches. Not until the 17th/18th centuries did work get started on restoration, continuing with excavations in the 1800s and this century's further improvement schemes.

16-17 If Romulus was the legendary founder of Rome, then the Tiber was and is the capital's putative father. For it is to this river that Rome owes her greatness. Through the centuries, as the urban area grew, so bridges were built to connect the two banks, and several dating back to Roman times are still in use today.

been opened to the public, covering a total of 55,000 hectares in addition to the 12,000 already existing. And to prove that smoky, polluted Rome is clearing its lungs, public transport is changing too: no to exhaust fumes, yes to tram lines. As in other European cities the once-spurned tram is back in vogue: admittedly slower, but definitely more environment-friendly. There is other more eye-catching evidence of the trend. Buildings and monuments formerly decaying due to age and neglect have been restored. Traffic has been banned from the Via Appia Antica, the "regina viarum": with its many archaeological sites and monuments, this most famous of Roman roads can best be defined as an open-air museum. Another sign of ongoing changes can be seen in the Imperial Fora, now open even after dark. Thanks to dramatically effective lighting, visitors can conjure up a magical picture of imperial Rome, with its profusion of marble, mosaics, giant statues, triumphal arches, basilicas and temples. In your mind's eye you can almost see legendary figures walking through the Forum along the Via Sacra: Julius Caesar, Cicero, Constantine, even Peter, a humble fisherman from Palestine, founder of the church that eventually became a symbol of worldwide renown. In the glorious city of Rome no time machine borrowed from science fiction is needed to bring the far-distant past back to life.

VIALE DELLE MILIZIE
VIA SAN PAOLO
24
25
22
VIA COLA DI RIENZO
PIAZZA CAVOUR
21
Spanish Steps
VIA CONDOTTI
VIA DEL
1
VIA DEI CORRIDORI
2
VIA DELLA CONCILIAZIONE
TIBER
18
VIA D. PORTA CAVALLEGGERI
VIA DEL CORSO
3
4
C.SO V. EMANUELE II
Trajan's Column
PIAZZA VENEZIA
VIA DEI FOR
5
9
6
VIA DEI CERCHI
VIA DEL CIRCO MASSIM
VIALE DI TRASTEVERE
TIBER
7
8
VIALE AVENTINO
10
VIALE GIOTTO

23
VIA SALARIA
CORSO ITALIA
VIA VITTORIO VENETO
DEL BRASILE
20
VIALE PRETORIANO
19
RABUINO
VIA NAZIONALE
Stazione Termini
17
16
IMPERIALI
VIA MERULANA
VIA EMANUELE FILIBERTO
Roman Forum
Arch of Costantine
15
VIA SAN GREGORIO
14
12
VIALE DELLE TERME DI CARACALLA
13
11
1 CASTEL SANT'ANGELO
2 VATICAN - ST. PETER'S
3 PIAZZA NAVONA
4 PANTHEON
5 THEATRE OF MARCELLUS
6 SANTA MARIA IN TRASTEVERE
7 VILLA DORIA PAMPHILJ
8 SAN PIETRO IN MONTORIO
9 CAMPIDOGLIO
10 PYRAMID OF CAIUS CESTIUS
11 BATHS OF CARACALLA
12 SAN PAOLO
13 SAN GIOVANNI IN LATERANO
14 SANTA CROCE IN GERUSALEMME
15 COLOSSEUM
16 NERO'S GOLDEN HOUSE
17 SANTA MARIA MAGGIORE
18 TREVI FOUNTAIN
19 QUIRINAL
20 BATHS OF DIOCLETIAN
21 ARA PACIS
22 TRINITÀ DEI MONTI
23 VILLA BORGHESE
24 VILLA GIULIA
25 PIAZZA DEL POPOLO

THREE THOUSAND YEARS AT THE HEAD OF THE WORLD - CAPUT MUNDI

20 The very beginnings of Rome and its history go far back in time to the famous she-wolf that suckled Romulus and Remus. According to legend, the foundation of the city has close ties with the story of Troy. It is said that Aeneas fled from his beseiged city with a few followers and reached Latium. There he met and married Lavinia, daughter of King Latinus, and founded a settlement called Lavinium in her honour. His son Ascanius founded a town on the Alban hills and named it Alba Longa. Later Proca, Ascanius' son, ruled over Alba Longa, and was succeeded after his death by his own son, Numitor. Numitor was deposed by his brother Amulius, who killed his nephew - the son of Numitor and sole male heir to the throne - and forced Rhea Silvia, daughter of the rightful king, to become a vestal virgin. However, Rhea Silvia was loved by the war god Mars and bore him twin sons. Amulius ordered that she be put to death and the infants drowned. Saved by a she-wolf, they were found by the herdsman Faustulus, who named them Romulus and Remus.

The story of Rome started nearly three thousand years ago, with seven hills and a she-wolf that suckled abandoned twin boys, Romulus and Remus. On April 21, 753 B.C. Romulus, by then an adult, used his plough to mark the limits, on the Palatine, of the place that Wolfgang Goethe defined as the "eternal city". According to legend, this was the birth of Rome. There is however some truth in this tale (and the she-wolf has remained the symbol of Italy's capital). Excavations on the Palatine do not conflict with the purported date of the city's founding. Remains of huts, walls, wells, shaft graves (discovered close to the Via Sacra) are proof that the fabled hills overlooking the Tiber saw some very significant developments. A tribe of Latins definitely did live on the Palatine and neighbouring hills (the Capitoline, Esquiline and Quirinal). The origins of present-day Rome are therefore right here, amid the remains of villages once inhabited by herdsmen and farmers. Having abandoned the swampy lands of their native Alban hills, these peoples settled in this strategically well-endowed spot, easily defended against attacks from their enemies, primarily the Etruscans. Archaeologists have even identified traces of the square site first marked out with a plough on the Palatine.

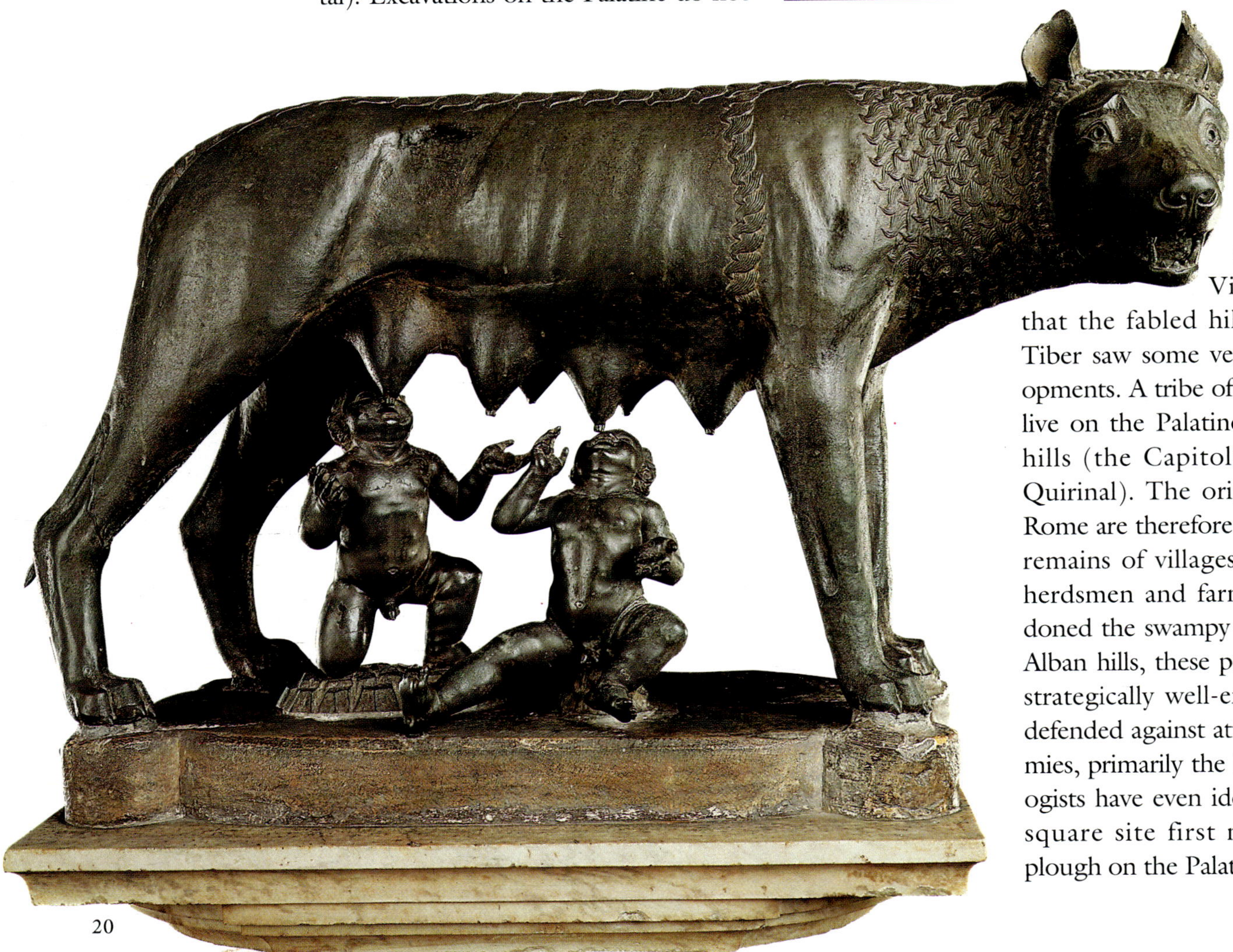

21 left The story of Romulus and Remus is told in stone in bas-reliefs at the rear of the Ara Casali. Dated around A.D. 200, this altar was a gift to Pius VI from the Casali family, hence its name. It is now preserved in the Pio-Clementine Museum in the Vatican. The carvings at the front portray Mars and Venus, the ones along the sides the legends of Troy.

How the name Rome came into existence and what the word means is not known. Maybe "town by the river"or "town on the hillside" in archaic Latin, or it might have derived from an unknown Etruscan word, but it was certainly not from Romulus, since his existence or at least his name is debatable.

There is however no doubt that the fertile soil found here was ideal for farmland (to grow wheat and barley) and the open pastures for raising sheep and cattle, while thick forests provided plentiful timber to build groups of huts, round and oval in shape, to house the community. Eventually encircled by walls built from mud and stone, these fortified villages became known as *oppida*: at the time of the first kings of Rome, in the territory of Latinus Vetus (2,350 square kilometres) there were about sixty of these settlements, each with its own fields, houses and defensive walls.

And one of them was Palatine Rome. These tiny city-states shared the same religious beliefs and long remained good neighbours.

21 right An old print shows the place where Rome was founded, on the Palatine and six other hills. Tradition has it that the city was founded on April 21, 753 B.C. by Romulus, son of Rhea Silvia and Mars and grandson of Numitor, king of Alba Longa. In actual fact Rome is believed to have been founded by the Latins to prevent the Etruscans from extending their domain beyond the Tiber.

Then, between the eigth and sixth centuries B.C., religious leagues formed by federations of villages attempted to impose their hegemony. Several became very powerful. The most important centred on the sanctuary of Jupiter at Albanus Mons: comprised of thirty tribes, it was led by Alba Longa, later destroyed by the Romans (legend has it that this victory was the outcome of the battle between the Horatii and Curiatii). Upon defeating Alba, Rome became leader of the federation. It is traditionally believed that Tullius Hostilius was king of the future *caput mundi* at that time and it is likely that Rome really was once ruled by a monarchy. Exactly how many kings held sway over the *urbs* is not known. After Romulus came Numa Pompilius, credited with founding the state and religious institutions, then came Tullius Hostilius and Ancus Martius. The last three kings were Tarquinius Priscus, Servius Tullius and Tarquinius Superbus: members of the Tarquin dynasty of Etruscan origin, they controlled Rome's destiny for about a hundred years (seventh to sixth centuries B.C.). Under the Tarquins the city became one of the most prominent centres of the Mediterranean area, comparable in size to a modern town: from 50 hectares and just a few thousand inhabitants, it expanded to occupy about 300 hectares with a population of 30,000. The residential districts spread over the Caelian, Velia, Oppio and Cispio hills and as far as the Viminal and Quirinal. Monumental buildings multiplied. A class of newly rich artisans and traders formed, a powerful "middle class" able to stand up to the landowning *patresfamilias.* It was in this period that the principles governing equality of

22 bottom The outcome of the war between Rome and Alba, the oldest city in Latium, was decided by a battle between two sets of brothers, the Roman Horatii and Alban Curiatii. Leaving legend aside, it is known for certain that Alba was destroyed by the Romans who subsequently became leaders of the Latin League.

22-23 top In this painting by David Jacques Louis, Sabine women intervene to stop fighting between the Romans and Sabines. After its foundation, Rome had to wage war on neighbouring tribes in order to establish its hegemony. The Sabines, led by their king Titus Tatius, retaliated - so the story goes - after their women had been carried off by the Romans.

patriciate and plebs were formulated. In the field of urban as well as social development, Rome was laying the foundations for her glorious future. The construction work undertaken by the Tarquins continued after their overthrow: among the buildings erected in the fifth century were temples dedicated to Saturn, to Castor and Pollux in the Forum and to Ceres on the Aventine, while the Regia and the temple of Vesta were restructured. The uprising that resulted in the fall of the Tarquins and establishment of the republic reintroduced old laws and the Tarquins beat a retreat leaving a new political system in place. The Etruscans however made a short-lived comeback: to avenge the Tarquins, Porsenna, king of Clusium, led an army from southern Etruria and laid seige to Rome. The Romans had to accept harsh conditions imposed by their neighbour.

22-23 bottom In this battle scene painted by Cavalier d'Arpino (exhibited in the Galleria Borghese), Tullius Hostilius is fighting the men of Veii. His name is linked primarily with the destruction of Alba Longa, then the most powerful city in Latium, and with the foundation of the port of Ostia, which provided Rome with an outlet to the sea.

23 top Tarquinius Superbus founds the temple of Capitoline Jupiter. This work by Perin del Vaga (1501-1547) can be seen in the Uffizi Gallery in Florence. Tarquinius Superbus was the last of Rome's seven kings. Under the Tarquin dynasty Rome became one of the foremost cities of the Western Mediterranean.

23 bottom Depicted with Porsenna in a fresco conserved in the Capitoline Museums is Gaius Mutius, a Roman nobleman. The story goes that, to break the seige of Rome by the Etruscans, he entered their camp in disguise with the intention of murdering Porsenna, their king. But by mistake killed the king's brother instead. Brought before Porsenna, Mutius admitted to his plan and burnt his right hand on a brazier as a self-inflicted punishment for his error.

In order to understand the events that followed the fall of the Tarquins some insight is needed into the way Roman society was organized at that time. Since the reigns of the first kings, the population had been divided into three orders: patricians, plebeians and *clientes*. They were also divided politically into thirty *curiae* and three tribes. With the end of the monarchy, the patriciate simply re-established their supremacy over the plebean monarchy of the Tarquins and excluded the plebs from political life by assigning them fewer civil rights. Appointed as heads of state were two *praetores* - later (mid-sixth century B.C.) called *consules* - elected by the *comitia centuriata*. The two consuls remained in office for a year. The first were appointed in 509/508 B.C.. During times of national emergency a *dictator* was appointed by the consuls, for a six-month period. The *gentes*, another important structural grouping in ancient Roman society, was a first step towards the population naming and identification system we use today. Members of the *gens* organization owned land and property and had acquired the privileged position and political clout to justify their leadership role: the plebs were excluded from political life. The patricians elected the city's administrators; they also formed the *senatus*, the assembly of *patresfamilias*' from the *gens* organization who acted as advisors to the *comitia curiata* and approved its legislative decisions. The patriciate's ascendancy over the plebs was the cause of a long internal conflict. Incidents such as the secessions to the Sacred Mount and to the Aventine forced the patriciate to come to terms: the tribunes of the plebs were recognized as inviolable and were attributed notable power in the form of the *ius auxilii* (right to assist plebeians threatened by excesses of the executive power), *ius intercessionis* (right of veto on any decision taken by a state authority) and *ius coercitionis* (right to bring penal proceedings

24-25 The subject of this painting by Cesare Maccari (1840-1919) is an episode connected with the Punic Wars. Cineas was sent to Rome by Pyrrhus to negotiate peace. Upon entering the senate and hearing the words spoken by the elderly Appius Claudius Caecus ("Let Pyrrhus first leave Italy and then we'll talk with him"), he described the gathering to his leader as an assembly of kings.

25 left The Capitoline Brutus was one of the first contributions to the museums of ancient artworks started by Sixtus IV in 1471. It is traditionally believed to portray one of the first two consuls elected by the comitia centuriata.

against anyone violating sacred laws). With the tribunates the plebs also obtained the creation of *aediles plebes*, auxiliary magistrates responsible for guarding the plebeian archives and treasures. These struggles resulted in the admittance of plebeians to the senate; in 366 B.C., following a rogation presented by two plebeian tribunes, Caius Licinius Stolones and Lucius Sestius Lateranus, they obtained free access to the consulship, in 337 to the praetorship and in 330 to the sacerdotal colleges of the Pontefices and Augurs. In 390 B.C. the city was invaded and left in ruins by the Gauls. The Romans built a new *urbs* on the same site: it was encircled by walls 11 kilometres long and occupied an area of 426 hectares, incorporating the Aventine. Major building schemes went ahead: the temple of Concordia (367 B.C.) and the construction of the first aqueduct by Appius Claudius (312-311 B.C.). Rome also acquired a new spirit: it fought and conquered nearby cities that rebelled against its power and, from the third century, began to expand throughout the peninsula and the booty of war was used to construct temples; some buildings were enhanced with objects stolen from defeated populations. Further building projects dating from this period were the construction of a second aqueduct (Anius Vetus, 272 B.C.) and the Circus Flaminius (221 B.C.).

25 top right This marble freize from the temple of Juno shows the Capitoline geese, which, squawking, saved Rome from the Gauls'attak.

25 bottom right The seige on the Capitoline hill by the Gauls ended with surrender by the Romans after seven months of bitter fighting and the payment of a large sum of money.

26-27 *The figures depicted in this tapestry, now preserved in the Quirinal, are Scipio and Hannibal, possibly the two most famous military commanders of ancient times. At the battle of Zama, Carthage suffered total defeat at the hands of the Romans. It lost its territorial rights over Spain, its entire fleet except for a few ships and was prohibited from declaring war without Rome's permission.*

26 bottom *The battle of Zama is portrayed here in a painting (1521) by an artist of the Roman School. This final clash between the troops of Hannibal and Scipio, in 202 B.C., marked the end of the Second Punic War. The actual battlefield was at Naraggara, close to Zama. Scipio defeated Hannibal using the very same strategy adopted by the Carthaginian leader at Cannae.*

lives lost out of a total force of 86,000). The Punic wars also left a mark on Rome's internal political scenario: two parties were formed, by the nobles *(optimates)* and the people *(populares)*; the period of office of magistrates, often engaged in long military campaigns, was made longer; conquered territories were established as provinces and became the property of the Roman people. A praetor was appointed to rule each province. In 149 B.C. Rome laid seige to the city of Carthage: a *casus belli* had been found when the Carthaginians breached the existing treaty and declared war on Masinissa (the Numidian king - and Roman ally - who had been provoking Carthage with encroachments into its territory). After six days of fierce fighting, Carthage was razed to the ground. The "battle cry" of senator Marcus Porcius Cato - *Delenda Carthago!* - had been interpreted literally. The concept of a universal empire had already materialized in the Orient when Cyrus the Great ruled a country that stretched from Iran to the Anatolian shores of the Aegean Sea, and was later further expanded under the Achaemenid dynasty. Now Rome the conqueror, unchallenged world leader, was the ideal candidate for such a role. The Romans were well aware their city was now a metropolis, at the hub of a new world in the making. It therefore needed to be restructured and reorganized.

27 G.B. Langetti's painting of the suicide of Marcus Porcius Cato, exhibited in the gallery of Ca' Rezzonico in Venice. A great-grandson of Cato the Censor and a supporter of Pompey, he was defeated by Julius Caesar in Africa and took his own life there, in Utica.

Shortly after the close of the third century came the Romans' hard-won victory against Hannibal at Zama (202 B.C.). This battle marked the start of an upswing in the fortunes of Rome. The Carthaginians were compelled to cede Spain, their entire fleet (except for ten warships) and all their elephants to Scipio and the powerful Roman empire; they were also prohibited from declaring war without Rome's permission and obliged to pay an indemnity of 10,000 talents. Zama was Rome's revenge for the greatest defeat it had ever suffered, at the battle of Cannae in 216 B.C. There the Roman forces were practically annihilated (50,000

28 top left
The amphitheatre by Pompey between 61 and 55 B.C. was the first brick theatre in Rome, it was restored by Augustus in 32 B.C. and later by Diocletian.

28 bottom left
Pompey (106-48 B.C.), a general and a politician of aristocratic origin, linked his fortunes with those of Sulla and fought against the supporters of Marius in Sicily and Africa. A consul with Crassus, he gained fame for having rid the Mediterranean of pirates.

Inspired by the *poleis* of Greece and the Near East, town planners started to build new quarters and to restore and modernize existing ones. Architectural styles were perfected (this was the period of triumphal arches, porticoes and basilicas) and building materials were revolutionized. Handsome public buildings were erected on the Capitoline, in the Forum and in the Campus Martius; pillars started to appear in private dwellings in the Palatine, Quirinal, Viminal, Carinae and Cispius quarters, while the first villas with gardens were seen in suburban Pincio and Trastevere. In the space of a century Rome acquired a new and distinctive face. The first great blocks of tenements *(insulae)* were built to house a swelling population. Growing numbers of people continued to flock to the city from the countryside, where they had no land to farm. Surrounded and choked by large estates bought up by Rome's prosperous nobility of mostly senators and knights, small landowners were selling their holdings - even for a fistful of talents - and going to Rome to seek their fortune. The urban situation was fast approaching disaster. And in the countryside, with the gradual disappearance of small independent farmers (an essential support for the Roman army), agrarian reform could clearly no longer be delayed. Appropriate measures were devised by Tiberius Gracchus, son of Cornelia and grandson of Scipio Africanus. Elected as a plebeian tribune in 133, he presented a bill to establish that no Roman citizen could own more than 500 jugers of land; in addition, any conquered lands available would be divided into lots and distributed to citizens, who would pay to use public land. He paid for his bold proposals with assassination. Ten years later, his brother Gaius took up the challenge: likewise elected a plebeian tribune, he resumed his brother's political battle and re-presented the bill. But, with his even more drastic propos-

28 right Lucius Cornelius Sulla, a politician and military commander of aristocratic family, is recalled primarily for the civil war against Marius and his dictatorship with its proscription lists.

28-29 When a matron was showing off her gold jewellery, Cornelia pointed to her two sons, Tiberius and Gaius Gracchus, and said: "These are my gems".

29 bottom Tiberius Sempronius Gracchus, a plebeian tribune who supported radical land reform was assassinated during an uprising in 133 B.C.

als for reform, Gaius too was eventually forced to admit defeat. Rome, meanwhile, continued to expand. In the second century B.C. a huge grain storage facility was built and this encouraged the development of a river port; other public-works projects included a covered market *(macellum)*, new paved roads, extension of the sewer system and two new aqueducts (Aqua Marcia and Aqua Tepula). This was the century when Greek philosophy caught on in Rome, although the ideas it spread were mistrusted by the Senate who saw them as a threat to Rome's authority. Carneades asserted that there was no absolute justice and that Rome's supremacy was based on the non-existence of absolute rights and absolute justice, in other words, on the (relative) rights of the strongest party. Greek art became thoroughly fashionable, as did Greek religion. All the Greek gods were adopted by the Romans, who identified their own gods with the ones on Mount Olympus (Jupiter was Zeus; Juno, Hera; Minerva, Athena). Commenting on all this Hellenistic fervour the poet Horace said: "Graecia capta ferum victorem coepit", i.e. "conquered Greece prevailed over her brutish conqueror". Fairly reliable sources put the city's population by 80 B.C. at 400,000. Significant episodes of this period of Rome's history were the first civil war between Lucius Cornelius Sulla and Gaius Marius, and the rule of Sulla as a dictator elected to introduce constitutional reforms. A determined supporter of the aristocratic party, Sulla remained in office until 79 B.C. Around this time Rome acquired an important new structure: the *Tabularium* (state archives) erected on the Capitol. Building and architecture enjoyed new favour under Pompey, one of Sulla's young generals who had won laurels in wars in Spain, against pirates and against the old king Mithradates. His building programmes played a determining part in defining Rome's distinctive polycentric configuration. During his rule work was started on the splendid Imperial Fora, following rigorous stylistic criteria (colonnaded square with the temple at the far end, perspective created by the axial sequence of the buildings) and completed some 150 years later. After Pompey came Julius Caesar, the talented army commander and statesman who brought Gaul to its knees and extended Rome's empire even into Britain. He had further buildings erected in the Forum and devised an ambitious - but never realized - city plan (its provisions included diverting stretches of the Tiber). Caesar had meanwhile "crossed swords" with his former ally Pompey, who disapproved of his military conquests in Gaul; he crossed the Rubicon and headed back towards Rome. Pompey and the Senate fled to Illyria and Caesar triumphantly entered Rome.

30 top *This bust of Julius Caesar can be seen in the Pio-Clementine Museum, in the Vatican. The great commander and statesman aimed to make Rome capital of the world and he redesigned its urban layout to comply with this vision. Plans were laid and work started on the Forum Iulium and Curia Iulia. Caesar's ideas included constructing a huge port at Ostia, draining Lake Fucino and building a military road from the Tyrrhenian Sea to the Adriatic.*

30 bottom *Antony and Cleopatra were defeated at the battle of Actium in 31 B.C. (a scene from the battle can be seen in this print). Octavian's ships, under the command of Marcus Vipsanius Agrippa, overpowered Antony's heavy fleet.*

30-31 *This painting by Heinrich Friedrich Fuger (1751-1818) is of the assassination of Julius Caesar. Caesar was not only Rome's greatest general, he was also a skilful politician. During the last years of his life he worked on preparing the foundations for a new universal and divine monarchy (a scheme later put into effect by Octavian).*

After annihilating the armies of Pompey's supporters and extending his authority to the whole Roman empire, like Sulla he proclaimed himself dictator for life, with the title of "imperator". How Gaius Julius met his end is common knowledge: on March 15, 44 B.C. he was struck down by a conspiracy led by Marcus Junius Brutus and Gaius Cassius Longinus. The conspirators, anxious to see the republic restored, were instead disappointed. Mark Antony, Caesar's ally, read in public the testament by which the statesman had left much of his estate to the Roman people: the outcome was an uprising against the conspirators, who were forced to flee. Meanwhile Gaius Octavian, Caesar's son by adoption, arrived in Rome (he had completed his studies in Epirus). Although only eigtheen, Octavian was an astute and accomplished politician. He succeeded in winning the favour of the Senate and turned against Antony. The two subsequently came to an agreement and, with Marcus Emilius Lepidus, formed a Triumvirate. After a war on the Parthian frontier Antony decided to settle in Alexandria; he fell in love with Cleopatra (repudiating his wife, Octavian's sister) and gave all Rome's eastern provinces to the queen. Octavian's response was an immediate declaration of war on Cleopatra, defeating her and Antony at the battle of Actium (31 B.C.). Cleopatra and Antony fled to Alessandria and committed suicide. Octavian took possession of Egypt. The days of the republic had come to an end, those of the empire were just beginning.

31 top In this painting by Antoine Caron (1521-1529), exhibited in the Louvre in Paris, we see how the artist pictured the repressive steps taken in 43 B.C. by the triumvirate formed by Octavian, Antony and Marcus Emilius Lepidus against the conspirators responsible for Caesar's assassination. Purportedly established for a five-year period to restore order after Caesar's death, the triumvirate was instead a means of sharing out power and eliminating anyone who represented a possible threat, for instance, Antony's enemy Cicero.

31 bottom left This bust of Mark Antony stands in the Capitoline Museums. Before he turned against Rome and suffered defeat by Octavian, Antony was a colleague of Caesar as consul and one of his closest allies. On the day after Caesar's murder, he held the funeral oration and, exploiting the dramatic content of the occasion, read out the testament by which the statesman left part of his possessions to the Roman people. The crowds rose up against the conspirators, forcing them to flee from the city.

31 bottom right The face depicted on this gold coin is that of Cleopatra, queen of Egypt. Her beauty caused a furore among the Romans. Antony went as far as to repudiate his wife Octavia (Octavian's sister) in order to stay with the stunning Egyptian queen. This step was used by Octavian as the excuse for waging war on his former ally.

32 top left Augustus Gaius Octavian, son of a nephew of Julius Caesar, became emperor at a very early age. Educated in Epirus to appreciate both letters and the art of warfare, he soon proved no less talented than his famous uncle. Under Octavian, Rome began the finest era of its history as caput mundi.

32 top right Augustus Octavian died on August 19 in the year A.D 14. After a month-long interregnum, Tiberius was appointed emperor. Under Tiberius, the figure of emperor changed: no longer eminens princeps *but* aequalis civis, *a citizen among citizens, with the same rights and obligations. He even refused to use the name Augustus and the title of* pater patriae *that went with it.*

32-33 The emperor Nero is traditionally famous for having set fire to Rome. This bloodthirsty individual killed his own mother Agrippina and his wife Octavia. In A.D 64, he initiated the cruel persecution of Christians.

In 27 B.C. the senate bestowed on Octavian the name of Augustus and he became supreme emperor and the senate's leading member *(princeps senatus)*.

Augustus reorganized the empire, establishing two types of province: senatorial and imperial.

He deprived magistrates and tax-collectors of their absolute powers and gradually replaced them with salaried civil servants. He also placed new emphasis on religion, and had many temples built. Augustus died in A.D. 14, at the age of 76. The new emperor was Tiberius, his son and heir, a wise and moderate man. During his reign, a pacifist - Jesus, son of Joseph - who preached the existence of just one god was crucified in Jerusalem. The religion he taught spread rapidly and before long reached Rome.

Here Christianity, like Greek philosophy centuries earlier, was seen as a threat to sovereign power. Upon Tiberius' death in A.D 37 he was succeeded on the throne by Gaius Caesar, nicknamed Caligula, who ruled for four short years. Tradition has it that illness turned this initially judicious and tolerant man into a bloodthirsty, callous despot. Caligula's aim had been to establish a Hellenistic type of monarchy in Rome: assassination ended his tyranny and Claudius, his uncle, took his place (and ruled A.D. 41-54).

Claudius was eventually murdered, poisoned by Agrippina, his second wife, who wanted her son Nero on the throne. Nero owes his fame primarily to two episodes of determining importance for the future of the empire.

He was accused of having set fire to Rome in order to rebuild the city according to his own plans, and he initiated the first real persecution of Christians whose proselytizing was producing converts even among Rome's wealthiest families.

33 top Gaius Caesar, son of Germanicus - nicknamed Caligula on account of the military boots he wore - succeeded Tiberius as emperor in A.D. 37. He was the first emperor to be chosen by acclamation by the army and recognition of the Senate, instead of being designated by his predecessor. Tiberius' efforts to renounce the godlike status of Rome's ruler were nullified: Caligula based his style of government on the cult of the emperor, representative on earth of Jupiter Latiaris.

33 right A painting of the catacombs, where the early Christian martyrs of ancient Rome were buried. Christianity had acquired growing numbers of followers during the reign of Tiberius. With Caligula came cruel repression, forcing Christians to keep their meeting-places secret and to bury their dead in underground cemeteries, the catacombs.

34 top left The lex de imperio vespasiani *presents Vespasian's governmental programme. A strong man of humble birth (his grandfather was a centurion, his father a member of the equestrian order), Vespasian devoted much of his mandate (A.D. 69-79) to agrarian reform, with the objective of re-filling the state's empty coffers.*

34 bottom left Vespasian met with a chorus of protests from irate small landowners throughout the empire when he decided to revoke the ius subsecivorum, *a law that had allowed settlers to take possession of part of the lands they had conquered. He thus reclaimed these lands so the state could then sell them to the highest bidder.*

The city was rebuilt under the Flavians but other devastating fires occurred (the Capitol in A.D. 69, Campus Martius and the Capitol again in A.D. 80). Vespasian and his son Titus restricted the area occupied by Nero's prodigious palace to the Palatine and the urban space was returned to public use. The imposing Flavian Amphitheatre (the Colosseum), one of Rome's most splendid surviving monuments, was built in this period. During Vespasian's reign, Titus brought the war in Judea to an end with the destruction of Jerusalem (A.D. 70). Domitian - successor of Titus, who died at only forty years of age - is best known for his ruthless repression of Christians. Upon his assassination a new system for choosing Roman emperors was introduced, based on merit rather than inherited right. Each

34 right By the time he acceded to the imperial throne, Titus, Vespasian's son, was already a highly considered ruler, thanks partly to his role in suppressing the insurrection of the Jews and destroying Jerusalem . His political life, however, became entwined with his personal affairs. He fell in love with Berenice, daughter of Agrippa I and sister of Herod Agrippa II. Her conversion to the Christian faith after hearing the words of St.Paul led Titus to adopt a more tolerant attitude towards the new religion.

34-35 In this section of Trajan's Column the emperor Trajan is seen offering sacrifices to the gods before commencing his war against the Dacians. Trajan, of Spanish origin, was considered Rome's finest emperor since Augustus and the Senate conferred on him the title of optimus princeps.

emperor would adopt his own successor, picking someone he believed had the necessary political and organizational skills. After Cocceius Nerva, elected by the Senate (emperor for eighteen months), came Marcus Ulpius Trajanus (Trajan) whose reign took Rome into the second century A.D. He received from the Senate the title *optimus princeps.* Under Trajan the largest of the Imperial Fora was erected - it still bears his name - as well as history's first "shopping mall". The empire's boundaries stretched further and further afield: Dacia was conquered and the victory narrated on Trajan's Column. Armenia, Mesopotamia and Assyria were also annexed and became Roman provinces. As his successor Trajan named Aelius Hadrianus (Hadrian), who left two enduring structures in Rome: the Pantheon and his mausoleum (now Castel Sant'Angelo).

35 top Trajan was an enlightened emperor. As well as addressing the serious economic problems of the empire, he introduced some important social reforms.

35 centre The emperor Hadrian is looked upon as being a humanist: as well as being an excellent soldier, he devoted his political life to maintaining peace and making Rome a rich, elegant city.

35 bottom Depicted on one section of Trajan's column are trophies won by Trajan during his campaigns in Dacia.

36 top Highlighted in this veduta *of Rome - on show in the Palazzo Ducale in Mantua - are the foremost public buildings of the ancient city.*

36 centre This 19th-century engraving offers a panoramic view of Rome at the time of the emperor Aurelian, with the circus of Severus Alexander in the foreground.

36 bottom left This reconstruction of the Baths of Caracalla underlines the architectural elegance and imposing design of buildings with a capacity for about 1,600 people, one of the most stunning structures ever built in the eternal city.

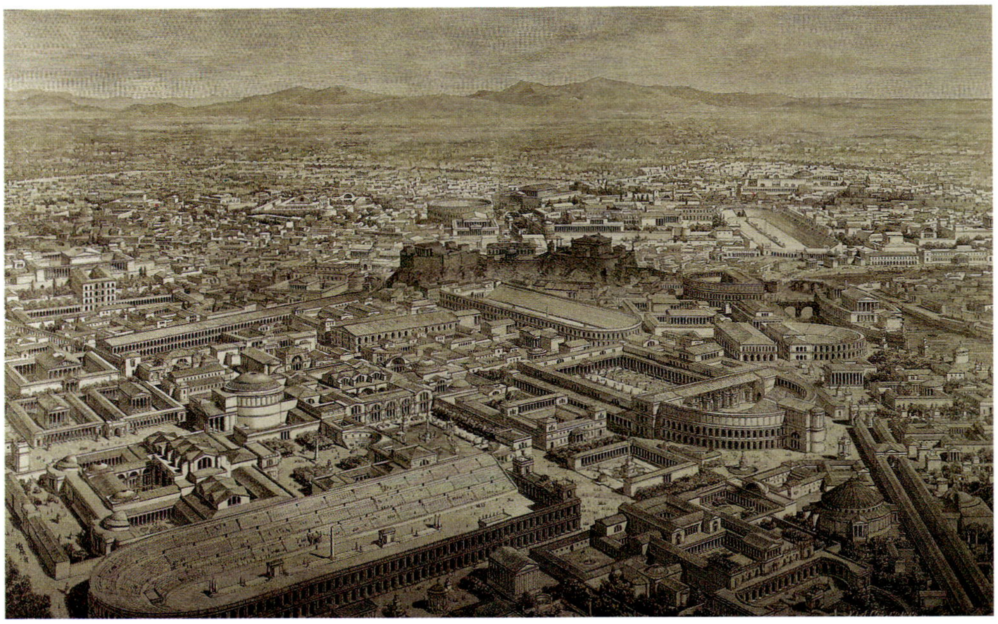

36 bottom right A plan of Rome by Taddeo di Bartolo (1363-1422), exhibited in the Palazzo Pubblico in Siena. All the city's most important Roman and Christian monuments appear on it, as well as Tiber Island.

36-37 A print depicting the Roman Forum and the Capitol. Especially when excavations were in progress in the 18th/19th centuries, ancient Rome had enormous appeal for artists who delighted in imagining what imperial Rome must have looked like.

37 top left
This picture presents a reconstruction of the Via Appia Antica, known as regina viarum *on account of its handsome tombs and splendid villas. Built on an existing route linking Rome and the Alban hills, the road was opened in 312 B.C. by the censor Appius Claudius Caecus.*

37 top right
The Forum symbolized the power of Rome and it was the hub of Roman life. People came here to do business, discuss politics and also - as writers of the time confirm - simply to while away their leisure hours.

38 top Emperor Antoninus Pius (A.D. 138-161) originated from Gaul. He was one of the fairest and most humane men ever to occupy the imperial throne.

38 bottom Marcus Aurelius (A.D. 161-180) makes sacrifices in front of the temple of Capitoline Jupiter. A writer and follower of Stoic philosophy, he ruled with his brother Lucius Verus as co-emperor until the latter's death in 169, after which he ruled alone.

38-39 In this painting Septimius Severus (193-211 A.D.) accuses his son Caracalla of having tried to murder him. Severus, born in Leptis Magna, was a valiant soldier and reorganized the state and created an absolute monarchy. Caracalla (whose assumed name was Marcus Aurelius Antoninus) was a ruthless emperor who arranged the murder of his brother Geta, his intended co-emperor.

39 right A porphyry column conserved in the Pio-Clementine Museum in the Vatican shows Diocletian embracing Maximian. In order to rule the huge Roman empire more effectively, Diocletian had divided it into two parts: the East (with Nicomedia as its capital), which he kept for himself, and the West (with Milan as capital), which he entrusted to Maximian.

39 bottom This bust of the emperor Commodus (A.D. 180-193) comes from the Esquiline. Son of Marcus Aurelius, an enlightened ruler, Lucius Aurelius Commodus was by contrast one of the most ruthless tyrants of the Roman empire. A man of great physical strength, passionately fond of gladiatorial sports and spectacles, he was eventually assassinated by conspirators.

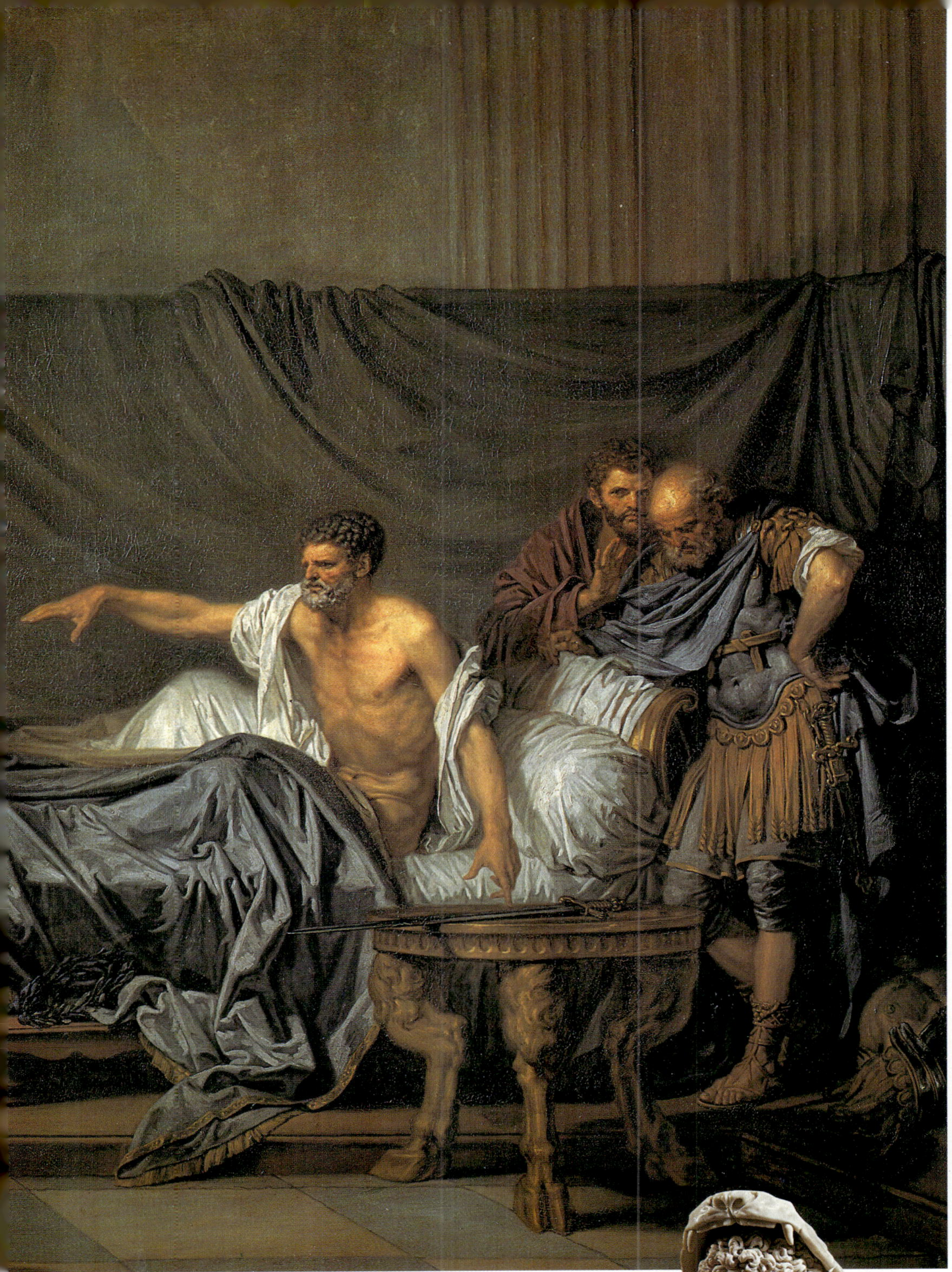

The man chosen by Hadrian to follow him as emperor was Antoninus Pius, a quietly competent ruler who, among other things, banned the persecution of Christians; he adopted his son-in-law Marcus Aurelius as his successor. Antoninus was a Stoic philosopher and wrote a book of *Meditations*; he was also long involved in battles with the Germanic Quadi and Marcomanni, who had crossed the Danube and the frontiers of the empire (in his honour the Senate erected the Antonine Column which narrated heroic deeds of this war). After the death of Commodus, Marcus Aurelius' son, assassinated in 193 by conspirators, came a period of political anarchy, followed by the dynasty of the Severi. The already shaky empire was weakened by absolute monarchy and ruthless struggles over the succession. The barbarians began to invade northern Italy and the Persians, in the east, conquered Armenia, Mesopotamia and Syria. Diocletian was made emperor in 284: born in Dioclea, son of an emancipated slave, he reorganized the state and established absolute monarchy, proclaiming himself "dominus ac deus". He divided the empire, firstly into two parts: the East with Nicomedia as its capital, where he himself was based, and the West, with Milan as capital, which he entrusted to Maximian, a military colleague. His next step was to divide it into four (a tetrachy), with another capital in Sirmium, watched over by Galerius, and one in Gaul at Trier, given to Constantius Chlorus. In 305, Diocletian abdicated and retired to Salonae. Maximian followed suit. The two remaining Caesars - Galerius and Constantius Chlorus - chose two other successors, but this did not prevent the state of chaos Diocletian's policy had been intended to avoid: countless leaders throughout the empire laid claim to the title of Caesar.

From this anarchy two emperors emerged: Constantine, son of Constantius Chlorus (proclaimed Augustus by the legions of Gaul), who favoured the Christians, and Maxentius (proclaimed Augustus by the Senate and people of Rome), who supported paganism. Constantine invaded Italy and in 312 defeated Maxentius near the Milvian Bridge. According to legend, on the eve of the battle Constantine dreamt he saw a cross in the sky, inscribed with the words: *In hoc signo vinces.* Constantine believed he owed his victory to divine aid and a few months later issued the Edict of Milan (313), allowing Christians to practise their religion freely. Later, in 325, he convened the Council of Nicaea, the first ecumenical council, at which the universal creed of Christianity was instituted. Continuing Diocletian's work, Constantine confirmed the concept of absolute imperial power, with the most important matters of state remaining under his control. Solely to decentralize administration the empire continued to be divided into four territories, known as

prefectures. Rome was deprived of its political primacy: the city that now symbolized the strength of the Romans was Constantinople, on the site of Byzantium. Rome's history in terms of urban planning and major building projects was now essentially at an end. During the two centuries (fourth and fifth) that signalled the transition to the Middle Ages the layout of the ancient "caput mundi" remained practically unaltered but its architectural face began to change as it adjusted to the needs of Christianity, triumphant thanks to Constantine. He had in fact made a first step in this direction with the construction of the cathedral of San Giovanni in Laterano, although its peripheral location saved it from comparison with great monuments of the past. No longer the centre of the empire, Rome was preparing for the new role that was to restore it to prominence in later centuries, as the city of the popes. Meanwhile, after the death

40-41 This fresco (dated 1246) in the Oratorio di San Silvestro in Rome shows Constantine the Great kneeling before Pope Silvester I. Constantine earned his place in history as the Roman empire's first Christian emperor; he also made Byzantium the capital of the Holy Roman Empire instead of Rome.

40 bottom St. Ambrose is portrayed with Theodosius in this painting by Peter Paul Rubens. Under Theodosius - with the Bishop of Milan acting as his counsellor - Christianity became the official religion of the Roman Empire (Edict of Thessalonica).

of Constantine and the short reigns of his son Constantine II and nephew Julian, the last great emperor to ascend to the Roman throne was Theodosius; in 380, to achieve unity of the Christian faith within the empire, he issued the Edict of Thessalonica. On his deathbed in 395 Theodosius left the empire in the hands of his sons, Arcadius and Honorius. The era of the great Roman empire was over. The Western part was invaded by the barbarians, while the Eastern empire survived for more than a thousand years.

41 top This manuscript illumination depicts the conversion and baptism of Constantine the Great. The emperor became personally committed to the Christian faith with his father, Constantius Chlorus, and his mother Helena, later canonized.

41 centre The Council of Nicaea (325), the first ecumenical council, met during the reign of Constantine. During its assemblies the universal creed (based on the Trinity of Father, Son and Holy Spirit) was adopted and the episcopal organization of the Church defined.

41 bottom The figure on this coin is Constantine II, son of Constantine the Great. He struggled for many years to gain supremacy over his two brothers.

42 top The pontificate of Adrian I Colonna lasted from 771 until his death in 795; during this period he met Charlemagne on the steps of St. Peter's.

42 bottom Leo III crowns Charlemagne in this painting by the school of Raphael. Now ruler of practically all Western Europe, the emperor signed a pact with the Church of Rome: in return for support for his rule, he placed numerous territories under the jurisdiction of the papacy.

Imperial Rome evolved into medieval Rome in a process marked by destruction and reconstruction. The political, economic and administrative decline of the State contrasted with important developments in the city's ecclestiastical structures. The pope became arbiter and defender of Rome, entrusted with its architectural heritage. Work began on building the first big churches: not until the sixth century was permission given to turn pagan temples into churches, after which the historic centre was appropriated by the Christians and the pope. The distinctive architectural features of the ancient city began to vanish: the huge public monuments of imperial days were abandoned or

42-43 The figures depicted on the altarpiece by Michael Pacher, exhibited in the Alte Pinakoteck in Munich, are the Sts. Augustine and Gregory, fathers of the Church.

converted to residential use; outstanding decorative elements (marble carvings, pillars) were "recycled" to build churches and monuments. Pope Gregory I (590-604) made the first real - and successful - attempt to provide adequate urban administration. Under Adrian I (772-795) much was done to restore the splendours of ancient Rome and the papacy formed an alliance with the Carolingian empire. The culminating moment of this alliance was on Christmas Day in the year 800 when Charlemagne was crowned emperor of the Holy Roman Empire by Pope Leo III in St.Peter's,

heart of the Papal State. The second half of the ninth century saw the papacy's first large-scale building project. After the Saracens had invaded Rome in 846 and plundered St.Peter's and San Paolo Fuori le Mura, Leo IV (847-855) built a wall to enclose a new sector of the city, on the right bank of the Tiber.

This area became known as the Leonine City, now the Vatican, a testimony to the engineering skills of its builders but also to the political as well as religious power of the papacy. The pope in fact became a kind of emperor, gladly supported and protected by Rome's self-interested landed nobility.

43 top This mosaic shows Saint Peter as he blesses Leo III and Charlemagne, offering the papal mantle to the first and the banner of Rome to the second.

43 bottom Leo IV, later canonized, occupied the papal throne from 847 until his death in 855. During his pontificate Borgo Sant'Angelo was destroyed by fire.

44 The coat-of-arms of the Orsini family. Together with the Colonna family (below), its bitter rivals, it was one of the most influential noble families of Rome. The new flowering of art and architecture in the city is to be attributed in part to the rivalry between the two families, who attempted to demonstrate their power through ostentation of their wealth and patronage of the arts. While Gothic style was spreading elsewhere in Europe, the characterizing features of Rome's urban scenario were tall crenellated towers and impenetrable fortresses, like those occupied by the Frangipane family close to the Forum, by the Orsini near the Circo Flaminio and by the Colonna in the northern part of the city.

44-45 Under Lothair of Segni, pope Innocent III, papal power reached new heights: not solely as the Vicar of Peter, but also as the Vicar of Christ and the King of Kings. This meant he had the ultimate competency to grant lands in fee to lay princes. The authority of bishops also declined and papal power was exercised by legates.

The urban landscape was further transformed in the twelfth to thirteenth centuries as noble, wealthy families added fortress towers to their palaces. During this period Rome established relations with neighbouring communes. The city's own communal government, formed in the mid-twelfth century, challenged papal authority and the increasing autonomy of the nobility. The troubled co-existence of papacy and commune did not stop Rome acquiring some imposing defensive systems. Of particular importance were strategic structures installed by Innocent III in the early thirteenth century, such as the Torre dei Conti and Torre delle Milizie, between the Forum and the Quirinal.

By now the Commune had occupied the Capitol and Rome was torn by bitter struggles between the city's two leading noble families: the Orsini and the Colonna. The pro-papal Orsini held strong points along the Tiber like Castel Sant'Angelo whereas the pro-imperial Colonna controlled the northern and eastern quarters, between Augustus' mausoleum and the Lateran. This partition had negative effects on development of the central part of town, until as late as the sixteenth century. Rome's days as a capital city did not end with the Roman empire. Admittedly, the splendour and beauty of the great *urbs* of the imperial era had attracted many visitors. But the arrival of the popes put Rome at the centre of the world again. Official recognition of its role came in 1300 when Pope Boniface VIII (1294-1303) proclaimed the first Jubilee Year ever.

45 top *Pope Clement V was French by birth (his original name was Vincent Bertrand de Gouth). It was in 1309, during his pontificate (1305-1314), that the papal residence was moved to Avignon.*

The city welcomed over two million pilgrims. And Giotto, called to Rome for the Jubilee, painted a polyptych (still conserved in the Vatican's Art Gallery) in celebration of this first Holy Year. Boniface VIII also founded the University of Rome in 1303.

In 1309 Clement V moved the papal residence to Avignon and Rome was left to its factional strife. Leading families ruled parts of the city and internal struggles curbed possible expansion.

While Florence was growing and blossoming during the Renaissance period, things in Rome moved in a totally different direction.

In the fifteenth century hardly more than 20,000 people inhabited the city, compared with as many as 400,000 at the height of the empire.

45 centre *Boniface VIII, born Benedetto Caetani, was a keen supporter of theocratic policies. On several occasions he was in conflict with King Philip IV, who wanted to tax the wealth of the clergy. In particular he issued the bull* Unam Sanctam *in which he invoked the supremacy of spiritual over temporal power.*

45 bottom *Boniface VIII, here on a coin, was briefly taken prisoner by Philip IV's councillor, Guillaume de Nogaret: the French king intended to bring him before a general council of the Church, accusing him of simony and heresy.*

46 top On May 6, 1527 Rome was invaded and sacked by the armies of German mercenaries in the hire of Charles V. The object of their attack was Pope Clement VII (Giulio de' Medici). The pope took refuge in Castel Sant'Angelo. While he was there in hiding, a terrible plague epidemic broke out and the imperial army was forced to withdraw.

46 bottom Charles V (1500-1558) inherited the crown of Spain from his mother Joan the Mad, and Franche-Comte', Flanders and the Habsburg states from his father Philip of Habsburg. He was crowned Holy Roman Emperor by pope Clement VII on whom, in 1527, he had inflicted the sack of Rome.

46-47 In this miniature from the Rosarium Decretorum, Nicholas V (original name Tommaso Parentucelli) stands surrounded by cardinals and bishops. This pope, a humanist and great patron of arts and letters, created the Vatican Library.

It was not until the pontificate of Nicholas V that the situation started to change radically for medieval Rome. He decided to move from the traditional papal residence in the Lateran palace and to build a new centre of the Christian faith, not a one-time centre of pagan worship. A centre with a basilica that would be pre-eminent in Rome, and a point of reference for all other churches. This was the premise for the future St.Peter's of the Baroque era. But also of great significance was the concept behind the pope's decision since its implication - valid for centuries to come - was that Rome had to answer to the authority of the papacy, and not vice versa. During these centuries of papal rule (ended with Pius XI at the close of the nineteenth century), many things changed within the Church. Its image as a single "empire" headed by the pope was sullied by the Lutheran secessions (1517) and the invasion and sack of Rome by the armies of German mercenaries in the hire of Charles V (1527). These were severe blows indeed for the ecclesiastical potentates. The Council of Trent, ended in 1563, confirmed Rome as the capital of the Church and the papal states enjoyed a relatively long period of calm, also on account of the papacy's declining influence on European affairs. The urban scenario was also changing at this time: the nobles, great families with

47 left Pictured in this very old illuminated painting is a session of the Council of Trent (1545-1563), convened by Paul III to ensure the unity of the Catholic Church and faith. The council met in three periods: the first (1545-1547) was marked by disagreement between pope and emperor over needs for reform and theological arguments; at the second (1551-1552) Protestant representatives were present, at the invitation of Charles V; during the third (1562-1563) the Jesuits Lainez and Salmeron obtained confirmation, once again, of the central authority of the papacy.

high positions in the church hierarchy, were leaving their centrally located residences and building villas on the hills (Villa Borghese, Boncompagni-Ludovisi, Patrizi, Sacripanti, Medici and, most prominent of all, the palace and garden of the Quirinal). The most notable contribution to city planning was made by Sixtus V (1585-90): he laid out new streets, repaired the aqueduct, and built splendid palaces. Among his plans was a series of straight roads meant to link villas and basilicas on the hilltops, from Piazza del Popolo to the Colosseum. The highest point of papal rule was the inauguration in 1626 of St.Peter's, the very finest of many Baroque splendours commissioned by the popes.

47 right Sixtus V (Felice Peretti di Grottammare) was the pope who made the greatest contribution towards architectural and cultural revival in Rome. He achieved great things in little more than five years. Not only did he improve the capital's urban landscape; with the aid of expert counsellors, he also modernized the economic and territorial structure of the Papal State.

48 top The troops of Napoleon Bonaparte invaded Rome in 1797. The French emperor made many improvements to the urban layout. Work started, for instance, on the construction of Piazza del Popolo. While Camille de Tournon was prefect, consideration was given to the idea of creating a huge archaeological park: restoration work on Trajan's Forum was the first initiative.

48 bottom Antonio Canova, using the earnings received for a commission from senator Falier, went to Rome where he lived and worked for a number of years. Among his most significant works are the monumental tombs he created for the popes Clement XIII and XIV. He reached the height of fame under Napoleon, a great admirer of his sculpture.

48-49 An unusual view of St.Peter's, painted before the present colonnade - designed by Bernini - was built.

49 top Here St.Peter's is seen from the rear. When Gian Lorenzo Bernini took over from Maderno as chief architect, he designed two belltowers to stand on either side of the basilica. Only one was actually built, in 1641, and it was demolished five years later after cracks appeared in walls underneath. The first basilica dedicated to Saint Peter was constructed in A.D. 320 by Constantine, on the site of the tomb of the apostle and martyr. The decision to restore the ancient building was taken by pope Nicholas V. Not until the papacy of Julius II, however, did the basilica undergo the restructuring that radically changed its appearance.

Two centuries later Napoleon described Rome as "the second city of the Empire" in terms of importance and charm. Although he rarely set foot in the city, he commissioned Antonio Canova and other prominent artists to study solutions for modernizing the old capital. Under Napoleon work started on excavations that brought to light remains of classical Rome, from the Basilica of Maxentius and the Baths of Caracalla to the Palatine and Via Appia Antica: testimonies of a unique era, that we can still admire today.

49 centre
This painting by Giovanni Paolo Pannini shows Piazza Navona, Rome's most famous square, as it looked in the 1700s. Already an integral part of the scene were the handsome features contributed by Bernini, the imposing palaces and the thronging crowds.

49 bottom This painting of the interior of St.Peter's is by Giovanni Paolo Pannini. Particularly evident is the totally convincing perspective achieved by the artist. The basilica occupies an area of about 22,000 sq.m., it is 186 m. long and soars to a height of 137 m.

After the Congress of Vienna, when pope Pius VII regained possession of the papal states, Rome lived through an eventful period. In 1849 Mazzini and Garibaldi saw their hopes of a Roman Republic dashed by the French general Oudinot; in 1861, with Cavour the protagonist, the Kingdom of Italy was proclaimed. Pope Pius IX, however, had no intention of abandoning temporal rule, in spite of Victor Emmanuel II's offer of a peaceful settlement. On September 20, 1870 Italian troops under General Cadorna entered Rome through a breach in the wall of Porta Pia. The pope had to withdraw and the papacy was left with the Vatican City, the Lateran Palace and the palace at Castel Gondolfo.

50 top left Giuseppe Mazzini (1805-1872) - seen here in a portrait by an unknown artist - was history's first authentic non-violent revolutionary. Founder firstly of Young Italy *and later of* Young Europe, *several times an exile, writer of articles and pamphlets, he was one of the triumvirs of the short-lived Roman Republic.*

50 bottom left Camillo Benso, count of Cavour (1810-1861), was the great protagonist of the unification of Italy. A bitter opponent of the Austrians and founder of the liberal newspaper Il Risorgimento, *he vigorously promoted his formula of "a free church in a free state".*

50 centre General Victor Oudinot, duke of Reggio (1791-1863), led the expedition that, in 1849, headed to Rome to challenge the Roman Republic governed by the triumvirs Mazzini, Saffi and Armellini. Along the way he came across Giuseppe Garibaldi. On June 3rd of the same year, after breaking his truce with the revolutionaries, Oudinet marched into Rome.

50 right In 1849 Giuseppe Garibaldi (1807-1882) led a group of followers in defence of the Roman Republic and won the day at Porta San Pancrazio, Palestrina and Velletri. After the fall of the republic, he took refuge in San Marino and then attempted to reach Venice by sea. Surprised by Austrian ships, he disembarked at Ravenna; his wife Anita perished in an ensuing combat. He made a further attempt to conquer Rome but was stopped by the army on the Apennines. Trying yet again to reach Rome in 1867, he fought the French and the Papal States at Mentana and Monterotondo.

50-51 On September 20, 1870, the king's forces under the command of General Cadorna entered Rome through a breach in the wall of Porta Pia. Rome too was thus annexed to the Kingdom of Italy. On May 13, 1871, with the enactment of the Law of Guarantees, the pope was granted full ecclesiastical freedom and the extraterritorial status of the Vatican and Castel Gandolfo was guaranteed. But Pius IX refused to recognize the law.

51 top Pius IX (1792-1878), original name Giovanni Mastai Ferretti, aroused great hopes among supporters of liberal ideas when he was elected pope in 1846, on account of an amnesty for political prisoners and the constitution he granted in 1848. However, on his return after the repression of the Roman Republic (he had fled to Gaeta), he adopted a hostile approach to liberal ideologies. After the unification of Italy he regarded himself as a political prisoner in the Vatican.

52 top left On October 24, 1922 Benito Mussolini announced the March on Rome to the Fascist Party Congress in Naples, on October 27 the quadrumvirs (C.M. De Vecchi, Italo Balbo, Michele Bianchi and Emilio De Bono) led the expedition towards the capital and on October 28 King Victor Emmanuel III invited Mussolini to form a government.

52 top right In this celebrated photo Victor Emmanuel III is pictured shaking hands with Benito Mussolini who has just formed his first government. The date - November 4, 1922 - marked the start of 20 years of Fascist rule.

52-53 Benito Mussolini is seen here with the governor of Rome, Prince Francesco Boncompagni Ludovisi (holding the ribbon). The occasion was the inauguration of Via Regina Margherita, on May 24, 1932.

53 left Benito Mussolini visits excavations in progress on the archaeological site of the Imperial Fora (April 5, 1932). The remains of the Basilica Fulvia-Emilia were unearthed during this period.

Rome began a new venture as the capital of Italy, one that led - in the space of only decades - to war and Fascism. In many respects twenty years of Fascist rule left as much destruction as the war. Convinced that the real history of Rome had ended with Diocletian, Mussolini demolished numerous quarters (with the loss of fifteen churches and numerous medieval and seventeenth-century buildings). One major redevelopment scheme (completed only in 1950, so the dictator actually never saw it) was Viale della Conciliazione: sweeping straight up to St.Peter's Square, it totally diverged from the original plan for a series of narrow streets bursting "unannounced" into the huge piazza, symbol of divine and papal power. Another of Mussolini's projects was the new EUR quarter, built for the international exhibition planned for 1941/42 but never held due to the outbreak of World War II. Another Rome landmark dating to the Fascist era is Cinecittà. The small "independent state of Italian cinematography" rose from the ashes of the old Cines film studios in Via Tuscolana, destroyed by fire in 1935: by 1937 the new studios were up and flourishing. In some respects Cinecittà offers a compendium of twentieth-century Italian history. The studios' initial role, in step with the regime, was replaced by desire for renewal, and determination to rebuild a country that had emerged from war on the verge of collapse.

53 top right Mussolini addresses the crowds gathered in Piazza Venezia from the balcony of Palazzo Venezia. For a while this building was the dictator's official residence and seat of the Fascist Council. It was from here that he announced Italy had entered the war.

53 bottom right Queen Maria Jose' of Savoy visits the EUR (Esposizione Universale di Roma) suburb of the city. Mussolini intended this grand development scheme to celebrate two decades of Fascist government and Italy's victory in Ethiopia. The international exhibition planned for 1942 never took place because of the outbreak of war.

54 top left In this scene from Roman Holiday *directed by William Wyler, Audrey Hepburn and Gregory Peck - the unforgettable stars of the film - are pictured on the Spanish Steps. The film was the first of a series of romantic comedies set in Rome.*

54 bottom left Giulietta Masina, Federico Fellini and scriptwriter Pinelli arrive from New York, at the height of their fame and fortune having just collected the "Oscar" award for their film La Strada.

54 right It is the most famous and, probably, still the most sensual scene in the history of Italian cinema: Anita Ekberg as she bathes in the Trevi Fountain beneath the amorous gaze of Marcello Mastroianni. The film was, of course, Federico Fellini's La Dolce Vita, *the year 1960.*

Italians were gradually putting the past behind them and starting to enjoy life, and this new mood was seen at its height between the Fifties and early Sixties, when the studios became an offshoot of Hollywood. With *Quo Vadis* and *Cleopatra*, the major American film producers brought in big-name actors, beautiful actresses, new ideas and - especially - the dollars that allowed Rome's young film-making community to spread its wings. In those days, when strolling through the capital, you might well have run into Liz Taylor, Richard Burton, Tyrone Power, Ava Gardner, Humphrey Bogart, Orson Welles, Rock Hudson, Audrey Hepburn, Gregory Peck and a bevy of other stars, drawn to Rome by attractive contracts but also by the charms of a city now in full post-war resurgence. Around this time three young directors, later to become outstanding exponents of Italian cinema, appeared on the scene: Michelangelo Antonioni, Francesco Rosi and Federico Fellini. From the early Fifties onwards Rimini-born Fellini made Cinecittà his permanent base. His exceptional talent and these studios - especially Studio 5 where Fellini shot most of his pictures - created films that helped to express and even to shape the Italian way of life: *La Dolce Vita*, *L'intervista*, *E la nave va* (And the ship sails on). This same studio (one of the largest in Europe, by the way) was used by Sergio Leone to shoot the interiors of *Once Upon a Time in America* and by

55 left *Elizabeth Taylor takes a break during the filming of* Cleopatra, *directed by Joseph L. Mankiewicz. Other members of the cast were Richard Burton, Rex Harrison and Martin Landau. The hoped-for blockbuster that brought 20th Century Fox to its knees was moved from London to Cinecittà. Rather than for the film itself,* Cleopatra *is remembered for its amazing sets, astronomically high costs ($45 million in 1963) and the troubles and scandals surrounding its star: Liz Taylor underwent a tracheotomy and fell in love with Burton during filming.*

the French director Annaud for *The Name of the Rose*. Beyond the studios, the streets and squares of the city have provided perfect sets for every kind of film. Piazza del Popolo, for instance, is linked with director Luigi Magni and his film *Nell'anno del Signore*; it was in Via Veneto that Fellini shot *La Dolce Vita* and *Le notti di Cabiria*. The Spanish Steps and Via Margutta were immortalized in *Roman Holiday*, with Audrey Hepburn as the delightful princess on a Vespa with Gregory Peck. The Trevi Fountain co-starred in the most celebrated scene of *La Dolce Vita* as a very seductive Anita Ekberg bathed in its waters, watched by an amused and provocative Marcello Mastroianni; the love story between Jennifer Jones and Montgomery Clift ended at the Stazione Termini; Roberto Rossellini shot the most dramatic episode of *Open City* - the killing of Anna Magnani - at no. 17 Via Montecuccoli. The Colosseum provided the backdrop for the legendary Nando (played by Alberto Sordi) in *Un Americano a Roma*, while Pasolini chose the working-class district of Testaccio as the setting for *Accattone*. The Rome we see today, the Rome portrayed in countless films telling of life and love in the eternal city, is also the product of post-war reconstruction. Now grown beyond all bounds, it is characterized by a historic centre packed with offices, a jumble of architectural styles, traffic jams that bring practically round-the-clock chaos to the streets. As the capital it occupies a key place in Italian life (with a population of about 3 million it is also the largest city) but its central political role is increasingly challenged. Well aware of its shortcomings, Rome looks to the year 2000 with a plethora of good intentions (lower pollution, traffic improvements...). It also prepares to welcome a major event of the new Millennium: the Jubilee. It is seven hundred years since the first Christian gathering organized by pope Boniface VIII, which also marked the very earliest steps towards the renaissance of medieval Rome.

55 top right *A scene from* Ben Hur. *For American producers Cinecittà became the new Hollywood. Rome's fame as the world capital of hedonism spread and actors and directors alike were on the lookout for opportunities to make films in the city.*

55 bottom right *Actress Anna Magnani, writer Alberto Moravia and film-director Pier Pasolini are pictured here together in 1964, in a Via Veneto café. The Sixties could perhaps be described as Rome's most stimulating years, a time of fervent cultural activity as well as self-indulgent pleasures. And the Via Veneto came to symbolize both.*

ARTISTIC WALKS

56 *Until 1981 the 2nd-century bronze equestrian statue of Marcus Aurelius stood at the centre of Piazza del Campidoglio, on a pedestal designed by Michelangelo. Since restoration, however, it is to be found on the ground floor of the Capitoline Museums, and its place in the square has recently been taken by a copy.*

Palaces, piazzas and monuments, but most of all, churches, dominate the architecture of Rome: each one a sight in which the spectacular element of religious ritual reaches sublime heights. Rome is an amalgam of art, history and architecture: it needs to be savoured slowly, street by street, as you stroll amid ancient Roman columns and past ninenteenth-century statues. Rome has a long history to tell: its fortuitous foundation by a community of herdsmen, the cultural and political centre of the ancient world, the survivor of nearly terminal decline in the Middle Ages, left to crumble with monuments of its pagan past by many popes but raised to further splendour by other papal patrons, the capital of Italy since the late nineteenth century. Every epoch has left traces. Visiting Rome is like time travel: centuries can flash past, sometimes in the space of just a few metres. On this journey through past millennia your attention will inevitably be caught by the pillars, walls, isolated arches and bas-reliefs scattered amid the verdant lawns that open up between the Capitol and the Colosseum. These are the remains of the Imperial Fora, once-splendid buildings destroyed, re-erected, levelled and dismantled again, their bricks and blocks

56-57 *Piazza del Campidoglio was the work of Michelangelo, who also handled the projects for Palazzo dei Conservatori and Palazzo Nuovo, on either side of the square. In 1940 Antonio Munoz redid the geometric paving, using a 1567 engraving as his model.*

57 top A view of the Victor Emmanuel Monument, seen from the Capitol. Modelled on the classical buildings of ancient Greece and Rome, this imposing structure was erected in honour of Victor Emmanuel II of Savoy, the first king of unified Italy. Work on its construction, to a project by Giuseppe Sacconi, began in 1885. However, due to the building's size and elaborate design it was not completed until 1935. The altar in front of the monument, inaugurated in 1925, contains the tomb of the Unknown Soldier.

57 bottom The Capitoline Wolf suckling the twins Romulus and Remus, founders of Rome, is a symbol of the city. The original bronze statue, dated to the early 5th century B.C., is exhibited in the Capitoline Museums. The twins were added by Pollaiolo in the 1400's.

used to construct more monuments and churches consecrated to other gods. With its business centres and law courts it was the hub of ancient Rome's political and commercial life, a meeting place for "lawyers and litigants, bankers and middlemen, shopkeepers and prostitutes, vagabonds and beggars" as the dramatist Plautus defined them. In short, the fulcrum of city life and a very evident symbol of the greatness and power of the emperors: each one demanded and planned his own Forum, possibly even larger and architecturally more stunning than his predecessor's. To appreciate the general layout of the Roman Forum it is best to view the area from above, on the Capitoline Hill. Extending below you will see the Via Sacra, used by generals for triumphal parades as well as for religious processions, the temple of Castor and Pollux, twin sons of Jupiter, and the one erected by Augustus to commemorate Julius Caesar, in the place where he was cremated.

59 top right Access to Trajan's Forum was through a triumphal arch that opened onto a square with a statue of the emperor at its centre. The complex included Greek and Roman libraries, the Basilica Ulpia (the largest and most flamboyant in the whole city) and a huge temple dedicated to Trajan. The dimensions of the temple have been ascertained from the height of surviving pedestals of its columns (1.80 metres), and from their 2-metre capitals.

59 centre right At the centre of the Forum of Augustus stood a temple dedicated to Mars the Avenger. It comprised a podium in tufa covered with blocks of marble, enclosed on each side by 8 columns (3 of those on the right side, 15 metres high, are still visible). Set in an apse were statues of Mars, Venus and - probably - the deified Julius himself.

59 bottom right Trajan's Column is one of the very few ancient monuments of Rome to have survived to the present day intact. Not only did its splendid carvings provide a record of Trajan's heroic feats in the Dacian wars: the large base of the column at one time contained the bodies of the emperor and his wife. Originally there was a statue of the emperor at the very top of the column; in 1587 a statue of St.Peter was placed there.

58 Trajan's Markets were one of the first commercial centres of the ancient world. Built to a project by Apollodorus of Damascus and completed under Hadrian, the complex was already in use by A.D. 107. Its construction was a hard job that involved cutting away a ridge of rock between the Quirinal and Capitoline hills.

59 left The column of Marcus Aurelius was carved between A.D. 180 and 193 Made entirely of marble, it stands almost 30 metres high and is 4 metres in diameter. Spiralling up the column are bas-reliefs with scenes depicting the heroic feats of the emperor in his campaigns against the Marcomanni, Quadi and Sarmatians.

The very finest monument today, preservation-wise, is Trajan's Column. Thanks to an intelligent initiative on the part of the local authorities, this and other highlights of the Roman Forum can also be visited after dark, when the ambience created by subtle lighting further enhances their impact.

Restored in the late Eighties, the column stands on the left of the Capitol, beyond Via dei Fori Imperiali. Rising to a height of almost 40 metres (including the base), this tribute to emperor Trajan is formed of 25 blocks of marble, each 350 centimetres across; its surface is entirely covered with bas-reliefs - 2,500 figures carved along a spiral stripe - relating the emperor's heroic feats during the wars against the Dacians (A.D. 101-103 and 107-108). The base of the column, 10 metres high, in which the ashes of Trajan and his wife Plotina were kept in a golden urn, is decorated with barbarian war trophies.

Above the door leading to the inner stairway is an inscription, recalling that the column was also erected to show the height of the hill levelled to make way for Trajan's Forum and the market complex.

In 1587 the emperor's statue on the top of the column was replaced by pope Sixtus V with one of St.Peter, the very first pope, as a permanent reminder of papal authority.

A triumphal arch right next to the Forum of Augustus marks the entrance to Trajan's Forum, possibly the most significant example of the artistic heights reached by the Romans. Construction began in A.D. 107 to a project by Apollodorus of Damascus and was completed under Hadrian. In terms of architecture and engineering it was a colossal venture: building the complex (300 x 190 metres) involved creating a hollow from a piece of land, 200 metres wide, that joined the Quirinal to the Capitol. While on the subject of record-breaking projects, among the buildings in this forum was the Basilica Ulpia (170 x 60 metres), with colonnades on three sides: it was the largest and stylistically most ornate monument of its kind built in ancient Rome.

Trajan's markets (also probably designed by Apollodorus) added a totally original touch. They were devised to support the Quirinal hillside, "lopped" to provide space for the Forum. In ancient times they were considered one of the wonders of the world: antiquity's version of the present-day shopping mall, with 150 stores selling everything from oriental silks and spices to bread and flowers, and space for offices too. The shops had arched entrances or portals with travertine marble surrounds; lining Via Biberatica, the main street, were taverns and shops selling spices. In 1200 the pope built a defensive structure, the Torre delle Milizie, over the markets.

The Arch of Settimius Severus,

60-61 An aerial photo offers an unbeatable view of the Imperial Fora. As Ovid recalls in his fasti *(Calendar), the entire area where the Fora were built was previously swampy land dotted with muddy pools and crossed by the Velabro, an insignificant little stream. The Romans clearly made an excellent job of draining and reclaiming the site.*

62 top The Arch of Constantine was inaugurated in 315 to commemorate the Emperor's victory over Maxentius at the Battle of the Milvian Bridge. The 25-metre high arch has three archways.

62-63 The Roman Forum was the centre of the city's public life for centuries. In this photo can be seen the columns of the Temple of Saturn on the left, the Temple of Antoninus and Faustina in the centre, and the Temple of Castor and Pollux on the right.

63 left The Arch of Septimius Severus was built to celebrate the 10th anniversary of the emperor's accession. Carved on it is an inscription commemorating the victories of Septimius Severus and his two sons, Caracalla and Geta, over Parthians, Arabs and the kingdom of Adiabene. Close to the Arch are the Rostra, the orator's tribune, decorated with beaks from ships captured off Antium.

63 top right It was the largest, most eye-catching and most incredible building ever to be built in the entire empire. But its size alone makes the Basilica of Maxentius (a basilica was the Roman equivalent of today's law-courts) one of the most stunning examples of Roman architecture. Started in 308 by the emperor Maxentius, it was completed by Constantine (who had since gained the upper hand over his former friend and ally) to suit his own tastes. A glance at the walls gives an immediate idea of its proportions: the aisle (35 metres high) and two naves were contained within a 100 x 65 metre perimeter.

erected in A.D. 203 to celebrate the tenth anniversary of this emperor's accession, has survived the passing centuries and neglect almost unscathed. Its relief carvings have suffered from the elements and pollution but you can still see the heroic Settimius engaged in battles in Parthia (present-day Iran and Iraq) and Arabia. Above, as well as the inscription commemorating the emperor, there were those of his two sons, Caracalla and Geta. After Caracalla had his brother killed, he had his name cancelled from the triumphal arch. An interesting aside: in medieval times there was a barber's shop in the central supporting arch.

Also prominent amid the ruins of the Forum are remains of the Basilica of Maxentius (in Roman times a basilica was a place devoted to business, administration and legal activities). Work on this imposing structure (100 x 65 metres and 35 metres high) began at the start of the fourth century and was completed by Constantine after Maxentius was deposed, following his defeat at the battle of the Milvian Bridge in A.D. 312 Rome's first Christian emperor changed the original project, creating a nave flanked by aisles with the entrance in the centre of the south wall (gilded tiles from the roof were eventually used to cover the first church dedicated to St.Peter).

No-one leaving the Forum could fail to notice the Arch of Constantine and the Colosseum, still spectacular testimonies to Rome's amazing architectural heritage. The first, with three arches faced with Numidian marble, was inaugurated in A.D. 315 to celebrate Constantine's victory over Maxentius. It took three years to build and boasts magnificent decorative reliefs, though none created ad hoc: its friezes and statuary were taken from earlier monumental structures dating from the reigns of Trajan and Marcus Aurelius.

The Arch stands on the fringe of Piazza del Colosseo, which occupies the valley once formed by the Caelian, Palatine, Velia and Oppio hills.

63 bottom right Prominent among the remains of the Temple of Antoninus and Faustina are the 17-metre-high cipolin marble columns of the pronaos. This place of worship was erected at the wish of the Senate, after the death of the emperor and his wife. Its good state of conservation is explained by the fact that it eventually became part of a church (San Lorenzo in Miranda).

64 Work was begun on the Flavian Amphitheatre in AD 69, under Vespasian. Titus, the son who succeeded him, opened it in the year 80. Between 81 and 96, Domitian completed the underground structures of the Amphitheatre and ordered the design of the barracks for the gladiators (Ludi) on the eastern side of the level part.

64-65 The outer part of the Colosseum was divided into four rings of travertine rock, 49 metres high. The first three of these consisted of square arches in half-columns with Tuscan capitals in the first row, Ionian in the second and Corinthian in the third. The fourth, of which only the northern side remains, has Corinthian columns that divide the ring into 80 squares containing 40 alternating windows. Inside each square were ledges that held up the wooden beams to which the velarium, the great canopy that offered protection from the rain and sun, were attached.

65 top left If we look at the inside of the Colosseum today, it is difficult to imagine the arena covered in a wooden stage and, underneath, all the rooms and passageways, which can be seen today only in the structure of the perimeter.

65 top right To reach the arena, there were two entrances at the major axes, known as the Porta Triumphalis and Porta Libitinaria. The gladiators entered through the first of these, to the west, while the second was used to remove the bodies of the gladiators who were killed. The events held in the Colosseum were gladiatorial combats (munera) *and simulated wild animal hunts* (venationes). *The first, which were first staged in 264 BC on the occasion of the funeral of Brutus Pero, and then developed to the point where they required imperial legislation* (lex Tullia de ambitu, *passed in 61 BC), were organised by an "editor", who promoted and financed the combats. The editor, who was usually the emperor himself in the late imperial period, negotiated the price of the gladiators with a proxy* (lanista).

Rising majestically at the centre of the square is the Flavian Amphitheatre - with St.Peter's surely the most popular postcard view of Rome. The Colosseum is unrivalled as Rome's foremost landmark and it is the largest ancient monument to have survived to the present day in a good condition. Commissioned by emperor Vespasian on a site previously occupied by the artificial lake of Nero's Golden House, it was the first urban space used permanently for entertainment. One hundred days of festivities and games were organized when this rationally constructed, oval arena was eventually inaugurated by Titus in A.D. 70. It could seat 55,000 and had no fewer than eighty entrances to ensure orderly flows of spectators arriving and leaving. Around the edge of the upper storey were long poles used to support the *velarium*, a huge awning that offered shelter from the sun, held in place by ropes attached to pillars that still surround the outside of the amphitheatre today. To add to the excitement, the animals were brought into the arena through trap-doors and in cages pulled up from three floors below ground level with powerful winches: early, elementary examples of lifts. History books as well as popular imagination associate the Colosseum primarily with the gladiators: these trained wrestlers - mostly slaves, prisoners-of-war and criminals - enjoyed the same kind of hero-worship from enthusiastic crowds as their present-day counterparts. But there the similiarity ends: for gladiators the rule was combat to the death. And the fate of the wounded and vanquished was decided by the emperor and the public. Even today Romans believe the huge amphitheatre to be indestructible (while the Colosseum stands, Rome will stand). It acquired this fame at the time of the barbarian invasions. The story goes that the barbarians made holes in the stone of its pillars and walls and filled them with gunpowder, to blow up the building. But the Colosseum just kept on standing, intact. The tale might be more convincing had gunpowder been invented at that time.... And the holes still visible in the pillars were actually left by crampons used by stonemasons when construction was in progress.

66 top The line of buildings on the Campidoglio - the Renaissance Campidoglio Palace, the 14th-century church of Santa Maria in Aracoeli and the white marble of the Vittoriano - sum up the long history of Rome. The hill where power was wielded from the days of the first kings of Rome and the cult of Capitoline Jupiter was practised, the church built on the foundations of the temple of Juno Moneta and the columns that symbolise the unity of Italy show just how accurate the capital's nickname of "the eternal city" is.

66 bottom The Senatorial Palace, today the headquarters of the local administration of Rome, is a building of medieval origins, restructured by Giacomo Della Porta and Girolamo Rainaldi to a design by Michelangelo, who had signed a contract for the new layout of the square. The tower that we can admire today, on which there stands a statue of Minerva, goddess of Rome, was built by Martino Longhi the Elder as a replacement for the medieval tower, between 1578 and 1582.

67 left This figure in antique red marble of a young laughing Satyr raising a bunch of grapes is from the period of Hadrian. Kept in the Capitoline Museums, it is a copy of an original Greek bronze.

67 top right The Spinarius, a bronze sculpture from the late Hellenic period (1st century BC) is also known as the Fedele Capitolino, as it was identified with Martius, the messenger of the Romans, who didn't stop running in spite of the torment of a thorn in his foot.

67 bottom right The Tensa Capitolina is a 4th-century chariot finely covered in bronze plate sculpted with bas-reliefs showing episodes from the Trojan cycle. This chariot was probably used to carry the gods in processions. We can admire the Hall of the Castellani in the Palazzo dei Conservatori, in the Campidoglio.

Rome was supposedly founded within limits traced on the Palatine Hill but the Capitol has always been the centre of city government. On this site stood the temple of Jupiter commissioned according to tradition by Tarquinius Superbus and inaugurated in 509 B.C. The temple, symbolizing authority, was the fulcrum of ancient Rome: all the most important religious and political celebrations took place here. Rome's local government still meets here, in Palazzo Senatorio, on the top of this hill. The Capitol is approached from the "Cordonata", a flight of steps designed by Michelangelo, flanked by two Egyptian stone lions, a nineteenth-century monument commemorating Cola di Rienzo, on the spot where the political leader was killed, and the statues of Castor and Pollux. Not long ago the equestrian statue of Marcus Aurelius reappeared in the piazza after several years' absence. It is in fact a perfect copy of the original. One of the rarest ancient bronze statues to survive to the present-day, the original has now been restored and can be seen in a ground-floor room in the Capitoline Museums. On the left of the piazza is the Aracoeli Staircase, with its 124 marble steps: it was completed in 1348, probably in readiness for the Holy Year in 1350. It was here that Cola di Rienzo used to address the assembled crowds. A seventeenth-century massacre also took place here: one night, Prince Caffarelli was disturbed by the mob of peasants who spent the night on these steps before selling their produce at the market next morning, so he ordered his servants to fill casks with stones and throw them down the steps. The outcome was a carnage (perhaps it was in memory of this massacre that the staircase became officially known as Holy). There is also a legend attached to the sixth-century church of St. Maria d'Aracoeli. It centres on a statue of the Holy Child which, reputedly carved from the wood of an olive tree from the Garden of Gethsemane, has powers to heal the sick and resuscitate the dead. The story goes that a very sick woman begged the monks who were custodians of the Holy Child of Aracoeli to let her keep it in her house for just one night. Meanwhile she had a perfect replica made of the statuette and this is what she returned to the monks, keeping the original for herself. The following night the monks heard knocking at the monastery door: it was a weeping child, the Holy Child of Aracoeli, come home. An ancient temple to Juno once stood where the church of Aracoeli stands now, and the church contains a number of architectural elements from monumental structures of imperial Rome. For instance, of the twenty-two columns, the third on the left bears an inscription: *a cubicolo Augustorum*, indicating it came from the emperor's bedroom. Other highlights of the church include a lavishly decorated ceiling - with a particularly noteworthy painting of the 1571 battle of Lepanto, commissioned by pope Gregory XIII - and frescoes by Pinturicchio depicting the life and death of St. Bernard of Siena.

1

68 top The enormous head of the emperor Constantine, kept in the Palazzo dei Conservatori along with other fragments, comes from the basilica of Massensius. The sculpture, which must have been around 12 metres high, shows the first Christian emperor seated on his throne.

68 bottom The Capitoline Venus is an admirable copy of the Venus of Cnydus, a Greek work from the 3rd century BC. The sculpture, with its refined beauty and sinuous forms, is in the Cabinet of Venus, in the Capitoline Museums.

Also bordering on Piazza del Campidoglio are the Capitoline Museums. The piazza is the work of Michelangelo, asked by pope Paul III Farnese to give a facelift to this particularly important corner of the city. The artist's project provided for a new building, Palazzo Nuovo, and renovated façades for Palazzo Senatorio and Palazzo dei Conservatori. Work started in 1546 and was not completed until the following century. Housed in Palazzo Nuovo and Palazzo dei Conservatori are the Capitoline Museums, the world's oldest public museums. They have contained a collection of Classical sculptures since Renaissance times. In 1471 pope Sixtus IV donated a group of bronze Roman sculptures: it included the Capitoline Wolf dating from the fifth century B.C. (Romulus and Remus were probably added in the fifteenth century) and a colossal head of Constantine, part of a twelve-metre-high statue originally in the Basilica of Maxentius. In 1515 pope Leo X followed his example, con-

68-69 The Dying Galatian, kept in the Capitoline Museums, was found in the Sallustian Gardens during the excavations for the construction of Villa Ludovisi, today the Altemps Palace. Believed for years to be a gladiator, it was recognised as a Galatian from its collar, moustache and the hair gathered into bunches.

tributing the Hercules from the temples of the Forum Boarium, and the Capitoline Brutus. At the instigation of pope Clement XII Corsini, in 1734 Palazzo Nuovo opened its doors to the public, the world's first museum to do so. The exhibits displayed in the old rooms of these palazzi are truly outstanding. Among the splendid examples of Classical sculpture are second-century reliefs of Marcus Aurelius: they depict him making his sacrifice in front of the temple of Capitoline Jupiter, during his moment of triumph and pardoning captured enemies. There are also statues of several popes. In the Sala degli Orazi e dei Curiazi, once the public council chamber, are Bernini's statue of Urban VIII and Algardi's statue of Innocent X. Prominent at the centre of the Sala dei Trionfi is "Spinario", a bronze statue from the late Hellenistic period (first century B.C.); the figure portrayed (also known as the "Capitoline Vassal") is Martius, a Roman messenger who completed his mission in spite of a painful thorn in his foot. Other exceptional works of art are displayed in the Palazzo dei Conservatori. For instance, the early-Empire Esquiline Venus, or the Capitoline Tensa, a cart used to carry images of the deities in procession: it is covered with bronze lamina and decorated with bas-reliefs of the Trojan cycle. In the same building is the Pinacoteca Capitolina, the art gallery founded by Benedict XIV in 1748. Not to be missed, in the Sala Cini, is a "St.John the Baptist" by Caravaggio and, in the Sala dell'Ercole, a gilded bronze statue of the mythological hero Hercules. More mythology and history is revealed by exhibits like the Capitoline Venus, a Roman copy of the Cnidian Venus; an array of sixty-five portrait busts of Roman emperors in chronological order; and the celebrated statue of the Dying Galatian.

On the southern edge of the Capitoline Hill is the Tarpeian Rock, traditionally named after the young daughter of Spurius Tarpeius, commander of the Capitol during the Sabine war (eigth century B.C.), and infamous since Roman times as the place from which traitors and enemies of Rome were thrown to their death. Tarpeia is said to have betrayed the Romans by allowing the Sabines into the citadel. In payment she asked them for everything they wore on their left arm, meaning their jewelled bracelets. The Sabines kept their promise, literally: as well as the bracelets, their shields were thrown on her and crushed her to death.

70 top The Appian Way was inaugurated in 312 B.C. by censor Appius Claudius Caecus. Work on extending the road continued and it eventually reached Benevento, Taranto and - in 190 B.C. - Brindisi. The first stretch is flanked by numerous monumental tombs, built in the republican and imperial age by prominent Roman families.

70-71 The ancient Appian Way starts outside the gate of San Sebastian, follows the Clivus Martis and heads towards Campania.

71 top The Casal Rotondo is all that remains of one of the splendid tombs erected along the Via Appia Antica by patrician families of Rome. In the medieval period the building - originally surmounted by a grave - was stripped of most of the travertine blocks that faced its walls.

71 centre This aerial view shows two of the most famous monuments to be seen along the Via Appia Antica. In the foreground is the tomb of Cecilia Metella, dating back to the last decades of the republican era; it was converted into a fortress in the Middle Ages. Visible in the background is the Circus of Maxentius: built in A.D. 309, it measures 513 x 90 metres.

71 bottom The Circus of Maxentius was part of a much larger complex that included the Imperial Palace and the Mausoleum of Romulus, Maxentius' son who died at the age of nine. Still standing are three sides of the portico that surrounded the tomb itself, a circular structure in the style of the Pantheon.

Viewed in terms of historic continuity, the Capitoline and the Imperial Fora are also the starting point of a road that has survived to the present day, in spite of the passing centuries and urbanization. The ancient Romans had good reason to call it *regina viarum*. The road in question is the Via Appia Antica which headed south from the city towards Campania. Initiated in 312 B.C. by the censor Appius Claudius Caecus, it soon became a popular site for family tombs and dwellings. This piece of Roman history has now been consigned once more to the people of Rome. At weekends, closed to traffic, it becomes a pedestrian area where archaeology and history buffs can pursue their favourite pastimes undisturbed, as far as the point where the Great Ring Road cuts brutally across the path of the ancient Via Appia. A shuttle bus service takes visitors from "Circo Massimo" metro station to the Tomb of Cecilia Metella, starting-point of an itinerary that takes in sights of outstanding artistic interest. The project pursued by the nineteenth-century French politician Camille de Tournon is now more than wishful thinking: sent here by Napoleon, Tournon had devised a scheme to celebrate Rome's grandeur, with an archaeological park stretching from the Capitol to the medieval hilltowns outside the city. Now with the Via Appia a pedestrian precinct, his challenging project is a step nearer to reality. In the 2,500 hectares of the Parco dell'Appia Antica you can now forget the problems of pollution and

72 top Porta San Paolo is one of the best conserved gates still standing in the city's ancient walls: constructed by Aurelian in the 3rd century, it has since been modified several times.

72 bottom Porta Maggiore began its existence as part of the aqueduct built by Claudius in A.D. 52 Not until the 3rd century did this monumental structure faced with travertine stone become part of Aurelian's Wall.

72-73 The gate of San Sebastian houses the Museum of the Roman Walls, a collection that explains the history of the defence of the city from the walls of Servius Tullius to those after the Unification of Italy.

gaze in admiration at the monumental tombs of Romulus and Cecilia Metella. Resting on the square travertine base of Cecilia Metella's last resting-place are a cylindrical structure decorated with friezes and relief carvings, and a stone plaque commemorating this daughter of Metellus Creticus, conqueror of Crete, and wife of Crassus, a general under Caesar in Gaul. Further along the *regina viarum* are other landmarks, like the tower of Capo Bove. Flanking the road is an almost endless line-up of ancient tombs; alternating with long rows of age-old cypresses and pine trees they continue as far as the Villa dei Quintili. Known as "Old Rome" on account its colossal size, this group of buildings was erected in Hadrian's time by the two wealthy Quintili brothers; they fell out of favour with the emperor Commodus who put them to death and confiscated all their property, the villa included.

73 top The single-spanned Arch of Drusus was built between A.D. 211 and 216. It is situated near the gate of San Sebastian and was used for the movement along the Appian way of the Aqua Antoniana, the aqueduct that supplied the enormous tanks of the bath complex of Caracalla.

73 bottom
The pyramid of Caius Cestius is 36 metres high and has a base of 30 metres on each side. It was the monumental tomb of Caius Cestius Epulonis, praetor and a rich figure from the Augustan age. It was built in only 330 days and bears witness to the diffusion of Egyptian fashion, after the conquest of that country.

74 top left *This pair of lions flanks the stairway of the Vittoriano, a monument dedicated to Victor Emmanuel II. On 9th January 1878, the first king of Italy died, and four months later the Chamber of Deputies, following the will of the people, approved the proposal for a monument to be dedicated to the hero-king. Nine million lire, an enormous sum for the time, were set aside for the project, from which the Vittoriano was born.*

74 top right *Piazza Venezia takes its name from the palace that faces the square, once the seat of the embassy of the Venetian Republic. During the 20-year period of fascism, the palace was the seat of the head of the government and the Great Council of Fascism.*

74-75 *In this aerial view, we can see the Altar of the Nation, burial place of the Unknown Soldier. The complex architecture of the Vittoriano, entirely in "botticino" marble, has often caused scandal among the Romans since it was built. As a demonstration of this, the local authority of Rome, in spite of the government's decision, never authorised the construction of the enormous structure in the Campidoglio, the "sacred" heart of the capital, and cradle of the Roman civilisation.*

75 top *Caravaggio's (1573-1610)* Rest on the Flight into Egypt, *kept in the Doria Pamphilj Gallery, is one of the early works of the artist from Lombardy. This painting is interesting for its composition and the figures of the Holy Family. The painter actually broke the almost sacred traditions of the holy image here. The Madonna holding the child is a simple girl who, exhausted, falls asleep to the sound of the violin.*

75 bottom *The portrait of Pope Innocent X by Diego Velásquez (1599-1660) can be admired in the Doria Pamphilj Gallery. It was this Pope, by means of a trust issued in favour of his nephew Camillo, who started off the great art collection consisting of over 400 paintings, which we can admire today.*

From "Old Rome" to Ancient Rome, we return to the Capitoline hill and Piazza Venezia. Overlooking the piazza is Palazzo Venezia: erected in 1455 for the Venetian cardinal Pietro Barbo, the future pope Paul II, it housed the Rome embassy of the Serenissima republic (during the twenty years of Fascist rule it was Benito Mussolini's residence). Dominating the scene, however, is a structure that could definitely not pass unnoticed: the monument to Victor Emmanuel II of Savoy, also known as the "Vittoriano" and the Altar of the Motherland (although Romans refer to it, more familiarly, as the Typewriter or Wedding Cake). Built after the death of the first king of unified Italy, to a design by Giuseppe Sacconi, it was begun in 1885 and, although inaugurated in 1911, actually took some fifty years to complete. Located here is the Tomb of the Unknown Soldier, symbol of Italy's unidentified war dead. Although a favourite sight among camera-toting tourists, this huge edifice in white marble and bronze is not popular with the Romans. Right opposite the "Vittoriano" is Via del Corso, which starts here and ends in Piazza del Popolo. This street has many claims to fame. Just off Via del Corso is Piazza del Collegio Romano and the entrance to the Doria Pamphilj Gallery, another of the city's treasure-houses. Among the paintings exhibited in its rooms are Caravaggio's *Rest on the Flight into Egypt* and Velazquez' portrait of Pope Innocent X.

76 top This wall with festoons is situated inside the House of Livia on the Palatine. Many scholars believe that the residence - famous for the decorations in the triclinium (false windows with landscapes scenes) and the tablinum (frescoes with mythological scenes) - belonged to Augustus.

Back in the vicinity of the Forum is the Palatine Hill, site of the very beginnings of Rome. As already pointed out, this is the spot where Romulus, raised with his twin brother in a cave by a she-wolf, marked the boundary of the city. Archaeologists have actually found evidence of Iron Age settlements here. And any gaps in verifiable history have been conveniently filled by yet another legend, this time involving the Greeks, said to have arrived here from Arcadia, led by king Evander with his son Pallas. Not until 1946 were floors of huts found on the Palatine indisputably identified as dating from the first Iron Age: but even in the days of imperial Rome a restored *casa Romuli* was believed to have been the home of the city's first king. The Palatine was once the home of rich and famous citizens, including Cicero and Catullus; Augustus himself, after his proclamation as emperor, chose the hill as his abode to assert his link with Rome's founding father. Transformed by splendid buildings erected by Domitian and, later, Septimius Severus, the entire hill became - to use a play on words - the "Palatium" of Rome's emperors. In medieval times this legendary site was abandoned and remained so until the mid-sixteenth century when cardinal Alessandro Farnese, nephew of pope Paul III, took a personal interest in the place: he built a villa here (partly dismantled in the early 1700s when excitement over archaeological excavations and relics was starting to mount); he also created Europe's first botanical gardens, burying the ruins of Tiberius' palace in the process. Designed by Vignola, the architect who created the interiors of the Chiesa del Gesù, the gardens boasted terraces connected by flights of steps, ponds, flower beds and trees never before seen in Italy. Most prominent among the Roman ruins visible today are Domus Flavia and Domus Augustana, respectively public and residential wings of the same imperial palace built by Domitian. Parts of the complex had two floors, others had three, depending on their position on the slope.

76 centre The Antiquarium of the Palatine, whose second room we can still see today, contains exhibitions of sculptures found between 1870 and the present in the imperial palaces and the forums. We can also admire the Domus Praeconum *and the* Domus Transitoria, *examples of paintings on display in the museum.*

76 bottom This fragment is kept in the Antiquarium of the Palatine. The hill was the chosen site for the residence of Augustus, as a symbol of the ideal union between Romulus, the first king of Rome, who lived in this place, and himself, the divine emperor. After Octavian, all the other rulers built their residences here.

76-77 The buildings in the valley of the fora began under Romulus and went on with Numa Pompilius who founded the royal palace, Tullius Hostilius the first Curia and Ancus Martius the first prison. Tarquinius Priscus intervened with restoration work in the valley, completed by Tarquinius the Superb.

77 bottom
The history of the excavations in the imperial fora began in 1870, with the work on the isolation of the temple of the Castors, which continued up to the eve of the first world war. The excavations resumed in 1930 with the work inside the Curia Julia for the removal of the baroque church of San Adriano. After a break during the second world war, excavations took place in the central nave and along the western side of the Basilica Fulvia-Emilia in 1946. The last year of work was 1960, when part of the Basilica Sempronia and the house of Scipio the African were discovered.

78 top left In the centre of Piazza della Rotonda, lined at the broadest part with buildings with eighteenth century façades, is the fountain of Giacomo della Porta, sculpted by Leonardo Sormani, rich in masks and dolphins from which the water pours out. The obelisk is that of Ramses II, placed there by Pope Clement XI in 1711.

78 bottom left The obelisk in Piazza della Minerva is the work of one of the last great Baroque sculptors, Ercole Ferrata, assisted by Algardi and Bernini.

78 right Since its construction by Marcus Vipsanius Agrippa in 27 BC, it has never been abandoned. The Pantheon, place of worship of all the gods of the empire first, and temple for the Christian faith later, has stood for over two thousand years. It was restored by Domitian and Trajan, rebuilt by Hadrian and completed under Antoninus Pius. Septimus Severus and Caracalla also made changes to it, before it was abandoned in 608, when the emperor Foca gave it to Pope Boniface IV.

78-79 The plan of the Pantheon recalls the ancient "thòlos", a circular shaped building typical of the Aegean civilisation. By comparison with the ancient construction, this temple is completely closed by a cylindrical wall, there is no remaining trace of the colonnade around the perimeter and a great tympanum portico forms the monumental entrance.

After the Imperial Fora, Trajan's Forum, the Colosseum and Palatine, there remains one last great monument to Rome's ancient civilization: possibly the most impressive, certainly the best preserved. For two thousand years the Pantheon has towered over the city's historic centre, only a matter of metres away from Piazza Navona and from Palazzo Madama, Montecitorio and Palazzo Chigi, the present-day triumvirate of Italian political power. This massive structure stands in Piazza della Rotonda, surrounded by eighteenth-century buildings that set off its austere and ancient splendour. The square, with its many outdoor cafés and eating-places, is a favourite stopping-place on tourist itineraries. The foundations of the first Pantheon lie two metres beneath the temple's paving stones and date back to 27 B.C. when Marcus Agrippa, son-in-law of Augustus, decided to build a temple "to all the gods", rectangular in shape.

Restored by Domitian and Trajan, it was rebuilt under Hadrian between A.D. 118 and 125, completed by Antoninus Pius and further restored by Septimius Severus and Caracalla.

Under the first Christian emperors it was abandoned. It returned to prominence thanks to pope Boniface IV who received the Pantheon as a gift from the eastern emperor Phocus, in A.D. 608, and dedicated it to the Madonna and martyrs. Over the centuries the temple has undergone many changes: in 1270 a first belltower was added, in 1626-27 another two - designed by Bernini - one on either side (the Romans, with their usual wit, were soon calling them "Donkey's Ears"); railings were installed to enclose the pronaos; in 1625 the bronze facing on the pillars was melted down by pope Urban VII Barberini, to make 80 cannons for Castel Sant'Angelo. Tampering and filching continued until Pius IX: he had the floor partially repaved, but preserved the original Roman motifs. In 1870 this temple of all the gods became the burial-place of Italy's kings (in 1883 the railings were removed, and the belltowers demolished too).

The great painter Raphael is also buried here. His tomb, beneath a statue of the Madonna by Lorenzetto (1524), bears an inscription by the poet Pietro Bembo: "Here lies that Raphael by whom, alive, Nature - great mother of all things - feared to be defeated and he, dead, to die". The most awe-inspiring part of the great temple is undoubtedly its dome. Created from concrete containing tufa and pumice stone over a coffered ceiling, the vault rises in decreasing rosettes to the apex and its *oculus*, about nine metres in diameter, the only opening in the whole church. The walls of the drum supporting the dome are six metres thick.

79 top The dome of the Pantheon has a diameter of 43 metres, corresponding to the height from the ground of its top. In this perfect ratio of proportions which creates a spherical form, we can clearly distinguish the definition of internal open space which was to influence the building of the great bath complexes and basilicas.

Also in the vicinity of the Pantheon is Piazza Navona, one of the world's most famous squares (in point of fact, an elongated oval) and custodian of an amazing number of works of art. Its shape follows that of a stadium built by Domitian (and the foundations of the buildings now lining the square were once stands able to hold no fewer than 30,000 spectators). Spectacle is still the essence of this site today since the piazza with its three fountains is a masterpiece of Baroque. The first of the three is the Fontana del Moro (named after Giovanni Antonio Mari's statue of a Moor struggling with a dolphin): the costumed figures, tritons and other ornamental features are nineteenth-century copies by Luigi Amici (the originals were moved to the gardens of Villa Borghese). Centrepiece of the piazza is the Fontana dei Fiumi, erected in 1651 to a design by Bernini (it was apparently thanks to this project that the sculptor won the favour of pope Innocent X). Rising high above the fountain is an obelisk, taken from the Circus Maxentius. Sitting at the corners are statues of the four great rivers of the world: the Nile (the head of this figure is symbolically covered to indicate that its source was then unknown), the Ganges, the Danube and the Plate. Until the end of the 1800s the third fountain was unadorned; then, for the sake of symmetry with the Fontana del Moro, it was embellished with sculptures of Neptune fighting with an octopus (by Antonio Della Bitta) and sea nymphs, putti and sea-horses by artist Gregorio Zappalà. Overlooking the square on the west side is the church of St. Agnese in Agone, built between A.D. 700 and 1123 on the site where the saint was stripped naked in preparation for martyrdom, only to be instantly covered by her own hair - so the story goes - which miraculously grew to hide her nakedness. The present building, erected in the mid-1600s (and completed by Borromini), has a traditional Greek-cross plan; remains of Domitian's stadium can still be seen beneath the church. Adjoining St. Agnese is Palazzo Pamphilj, built by Girolamo Rinaldi between 1644 and 1650: it now houses the Brazilian Embassy and the Italo-Brazilian Cultural Centre.

80 Piazza Navona was built on the site of the stadium of Domitian. The layout of the square actually recalls the form of this sports complex.

80-81 Piazza Navona is believed to take its name from the fact that the "agones", or sporting contests, took place here in ancient times. From this the name was distorted to "n'agone" and then through Navone to the Navona of today.

81 top left At the corners of the Baroque architectural composition of the Fontana dei Quattro Fiumi (Fountain of the Four Rivers), are the gigantic personifications of the greatest rivers on earth: the Nile, by Giacomo Antonio Facelli, the Ganges by Claude Poussin, the Danube by Antonio Raggi and the River Plate by Francesco Baratta.

81 top right Built to honour the Pamphilj family, the Fontana dei Quattro Fiumi in Piazza Navona was completed by Gian Lorenzo Bernini in 1651, a year after the date set. Pope Innocent X Pamphilj wanted the work to be opened in 1650, on the occasion of the Jubilee.

82 top The Column of Marcus Aurelius, erected in 180-193, tells the story of the emperor's deeds against the Marcomanian, Qudric and Sarmatian peoples.

82 bottom Via Sistina is the street that links Trinità dei Monti with Piazza Barberini. Here we find the Sistine Theatre and the Baroque church of Saints Ildefonso and Thomas of Villanova.

82-83 Via della Croce is one of the streets that run from Via del Corso to Piazza di Spagna, or the Spanish Steps.

83 top left The fruit and vegetable market has been in Campo de' Fiori since 1869. In this square took place games, horse races and executions. One of the best known was the execution of Giordano Bruno, a philosopher burned alive on 17th February 1600.

83 top right A few nuns have made their shopping in Campo de' Fiori. According to tradition, the name of the square derives from Flora, the woman loved by Pompey.

VIA
BOCCA DI LEONE
DIVIETO
DI FERMATA

30
31

85 top right
The cloister of the church of the Santi Quattro Coronati (Four Crowned Saints), dedicated to the soldiers Severo, has the labrum of Pasquale II in the centre and early Christian and Roman inscriptions on the walls.

85 bottom right
This garden is in Via Margutta, the street famous as the meeting place for Italian and foreign artists from the end of the 17th century onwards.

84-85 The old houses of Rome with their special fascination have been the residences of many celebrities in the course of the centuries. Some of these houses were demolished during town planning renovations. Goethe lived in Via del Corso, Mozart in a building that no longer exists in Piazza Nicosia, Raphael in Piazza Scossacavalli, where he died, and in Via Coronari, Wagner in Via del Babuino and Bernini on the corner of Via Propaganda Fide and Via della Mercede.

85 top left
This photograph shows the entrance to San Silvestro in Capite. It is so called because the building contains a fragment of the head of John the Baptist.

85 bottom left
This courtyard faces onto Via di Monserrato. In this street, which leads to Piazza Farnese, is the church of San Gerolamo della Carità. Here, San Filippo Neri founded his institute and lived in the nearby monastery.

86 top left In this aerial view we can recognise Trinità dei Monti and the Spanish Steps. The current layout of the square took shape between the 15th and 19th centuries.

86 top right Not many people know that the water that flows in the Barcaccia, the boat-shaped fountain in front of the Spanish Steps, is drinkable. Commissioned from Pietro Bernini, the father of Gian Lorenzo, by Pope Urban VIII Barberini in 1629, this shows a stone boat that looks as if it is floating in a tank beneath the level of the square. In this way, Bernini solved the problem of water pressure, which is rather low at this point.

86-87 Near Via dei Condotti, one of the most famous shopping streets in the world, are the Spanish Steps, with Trinità dei Monti appearing at the top of the stairway used as a backdrop for films and fashion parades. Begun in 1495 under Charles VIII, it was consecrated by Sistus V in 1585, two years after Domenico Fontana had been commissioned with the double access stairway.

87 top Students, tourists and office workers often come here to take a walk or to sit and enjoy the beauty of the Spanish Steps. The butterfly-shaped square was initially known as Platea Trinitatis, then one half came to be known as "Di Spagna", as the Spanish ambassador lived there, and the other, at the Via del Babuino side, "Di Francia", as this was the site of the French embassy. A major meeting point due to the presence of the two superpowers, this square became the meeting place and point of attraction for the Roman intellectuals in the 16th century, with the residences of writers and artists and many hotels and boarding houses.

87 bottom Via dei Condotti takes its name from the water supply network of the Aqua Virgo, or virgin water, built by Agrippa in 19 BC. This famous street of chic boutiques also contains the church of the Holy Trinity of the Spaniards, built together with the convent attached to it between 1741 and 1746 by Emanuel Rodriguez de Santos.

Heading north-east from Piazza Navona you come to Piazza di Spagna, the other best-known and much frequented part of the city, with nearby Via Condotti, home of chic boutiques that are a high spot on the Roman fashion scene. It was in the Fifties and Sixties - the period of Federico Fellini's *La Dolce Vita* - that this corner of the capital staked its claim to fame. Rome was then perceived, internationally, as the place where it was all "happening": exemplifying the ultimate in alluring lifestyles, it attracted pleasure-seeking tourists, drawn by the potential excitement of hot summer nights. This was the Rome celebrated by top film directors and actors of the day and further glamourized by Hollywood stars. Together with the Trevi Fountain, Piazza Navona and Piazza di Spagna have, in a way, remained symbols of Rome's heydey in those post-war years. And they continue to attract admirers from all over the globe. Piazza di Spagna took shape over a period of 400 years, between the fifteenth and nineteenth centuries. Dominated by the church of Trinità dei Monti, it was initially known as "platea Trinitatis" but later named after the Palazzo di Spagna, built here in the seventeenth century to house the Spanish Embassy to the Holy See (the whole area was in fact controlled by Spanish governors and access was not easy). The two foremost features of this outstanding part of the urban landscape are the Barcaccia Fountain, commissioned by pope Urbano VIII Barberini and designed by Pietro Bernini in 1629, and the Spanish Steps, a splendid Baroque structure by Francesco De Sanctis for pope Innocent XIII. Prominent on the corner of the Spanish Steps is a small red house where the English Romantic poet John Keats died in 1821. Suffering from consumption and his unresolved love for Fanny Brawne, he had been sent to Rome by his doctors, in November 1820, to breathe the air of Rome. Today the building houses a foundation and library honouring the English Romantic poets. The great German writer, Johann Wolfgang Goethe, also lived close to Piazza di Spagna, in Via del Corso. It was during the two years he spent here, from 1786 to 1788, that he wrote his *Italienische Reise*.

88 top The Obelisk of Flaminius in Piazza del Popolo has four white marble lion-fountains in Egyptian style, built by Giuseppe Valadier under the prefecture of Camillo de Tournon.

88 centre Piazza del Popolo was the inspiration behind many Baroque works in Europe. The southern side of this large square opens up into three axes - Via di Ripetta, Via del Corso and Via del Babuino - which all converge on the obelisk and head towards the city centre. This urban design is known as the "Renaissance Trident".

88 bottom The twin churches of Santa Maria dei Miracoli and Santa Maria di Montesanto in Piazza del Popolo are not in fact identical, the perspective only makes them seem to be the same size. They were begun one after the other at the end of the 17th century, then completed and embellished by Gian Lorenzo Bernini (Santa Maria di Montesanto) and Carlo Fontana (Santa Maria dei Miracoli).

88-89 The Flaminian Obelisk is the highest - 36.5 metres including the base - and the oldest in Rome after the Lateran one. It is a granite monolith from Heliopolis, built on the orders of Ramses II and his son Mineptah in 1200 BC. It was taken to Rome by Augustus, who positioned it in the Circus Maximum. Its current location is due to Sistus V in 1589.

89 left The Ara Pacis Augustae bears witness to the period of the most famous Roman emperor, and celebrates the peace imposed after the enterprises of the Roman legions in Gaul and Spain. The Augustan gesture, the royal family, and even an Aeneas with the sow and thirty piglets, are the themes of the bas-reliefs. The altar was found in the ancient Via Lata - now Via del Corso - and placed in its modern position in 1938, on the occasion of the two thousandth anniversary of Augustus.

89 right This photo shows the procession of the imperial family for the vow on the altar, in the bas-relief of the Ara Pacis Augustae. Among the sculpted figures we can see Augustus, Agrippa, Julia and Tiberius.

In the 1700s the whole area around Piazza di Spagna was full of hotels. They were not only frequented by illustrious foreign travellers like Goethe and other writers of the period: guests included many pilgrims too. The church of Trinità dei Monti was on an alternative route developed in the sixteenth century to accommodate the pilgrims who flocked in growing numbers to the great shrine of the Christian faith. The route started from Piazza del Popolo, with the twin churches of St. Maria di Montesano and St. Maria dei Miracoli, and the adjoining Pincio Gardens, where the Romans traditionally meet and go for strolls. The Vatican City is only a short distance away.

In this direction, on the banks of the Tiber, stands a monument of exceptional archaeological importance: the Ara Pacis (Altar of Peace) celebrates the peace created throughout the Mediterranean by Augustus, with his victories over the Gauls and in Spain. Commissioned by the Senate in 13 B.C., the altar took four years to build.

It stands in a square enclosure (also protected by glass) and is decorated with low-relief carvings of such high quality it is thought the craftsmen may have been Greeks; among the scenes so realistically depicted is the procession held to mark the dedication of the altar, in which members of the emperor's family can be identified.

91 top left The Trevi Fountain became even more famous with the film La Dolce Vita *This image of a hedonistic, uninhibited Rome was the stereotype of the Italian lifestyle for many years.*

91 top right The square that houses the Trevi Fountain is semi-circular in shape and extremely elegant. Well worth a look is the 17th-century church of St. Vincent and Anastasio, with its complex colonnaded façade, which earned it the nickname il canneto *(the reed bed).*

90 Giacomo Della Porta, Gian Lorenzo Bernini, Pietro da Cortona, Carlo Fontana, Pietro Bracci, sculptor of the Statue of the Ocean, and Nicola Salvi (designer), all the major artistic names of Rome at the time, worked on the Trevi Fountain in the first half of the 18th century. This monument was built on behalf of Clement XII and takes its name from the "trivio", or meeting place of three streets, in Piazza dei Crociferi. The imposing monument covers a whole side of the Palazzo Poli (20 metres long and 26 high).

90-91 Now it is a ritual - everyone who passes through Piazza di Trevi, whether they be tourists or superstitious Romans, have to throw a coin into the fountain. It is said that a coin donated to this famous Roman monument brings good luck and means that you will come back to the Eternal City one day. Coins apart, the most picturesque of the Roman fountains has other powers - according to the tradition, if two lovers drink the water of the fountain and break the glass on its stones, their love will be everlasting.

St.Peter's and the Vatican are now close at hand. But Rome has other sights to reveal before you cross the Tiber and enter the amazing world of art and culture enclosed within this small State, and the smaller, delightfully proletarian quarter of Trastevere. The last of the trio that contributed so much to the prevailing Sixties image of the eternal city is, of course, the Trevi Fountain, a grandiose monument within yards of Palazzo Quirinale, which is guarded by huge statues of Castor and Pollux. Compared with other Roman monuments, the fountain is a recent acquisition, completed in 1762 during the papacy of Clement XIII.

The site for the monument designed by Nicola Salvi - next to Palazzo Poli - was not picked at random: it was originally the terminal of the Aqua Virgo aqueduct, built by Agrippa in 19 B.C., and a statue in one of the first-storey niches in fact shows a girl pointing to the water's spring. The central figure is Neptune, on a chariot drawn by tritons and sea-horses, while the eye-catching forms of Salubrity and Abundance occupy two side recesses. Tradition dictates that you toss a coin into the fountain, to ensure your return to Rome. And it was right here that Fellini filmed the memorable scene from *La Dolce Vita* in which Anita Ekberg, wearing a black dress that hugged her equally memorable curves, bathed in the waters under Neptune's gaze.

92 top *The statue of Ares Ludovisi is in Palazzo Altemps, part of the National Museum of Rome. This is believed to be the Roman copy of a Greek original, and it was restored by Gian Lorenzo Bernini in 1622.*

92 bottom *This head of Antinous is in the first floor of the National Roman Museum. This is one of the most important collections of ancient art in the world.*

92-93 *The Great Ludovisi, displayed in Palazzo Altemps, is a bas-relief sculpted sarcophagus. The front is structured on three levels, with the victors on top, the combatants in the middle and the defeated barbarians at the bottom.*

93 left *The Group of the Suicidal Galatian is also kept in Palazzo Altemps. This was discovered in the 17th century, during the construction of Villa Ludovisi, on the site of the residence of Julius Caesar and later Sallust. It may form part of a composition for Attalus, 1st king of Pergamon, to decorate the temple of Athena Nikephoros, in memory of his victory over the Galatians.*

This seems an appropriate point for a brief digression on the amazing legacy Rome offers to art lovers. The city has more than sixty museums and art galleries. Prominent amongst them are the Museo Nazionale Romano and Palazzo Altemps. The Museo Nazionale Romano contains one of the world's largest archaeological collections, now divided between a building in the Diocletian Baths and (since 1889) Collegio Massimo. Palazzo Altemps is the home of the Ludovisi collection. Its most spectacular exhibits include the Ludovisi throne with its relief carvings, discovered in the late nineteenth century during construction of the Ludovisi quarter; the Galatian portrayed as he kills himself and his wife; the amazing head of Hera, also known as the *Ludovisi Juno* and considered one of the finest sculptures of all time; the *Boxer* and *Aphrodite* (first century B.C.).

93 top right
This fragment of the throne of Ludovisi in Palazzo Altemps shows the birth of Aphrodite. The myth says that Kronos cut off the genitals of his father Uranus with a diamond and threw them into the sea. They remained in the midst of the currents for a long time, producing a white foam from which Aphrodite was born.

93 bottom right
This copy of the discus thrower by Miro is kept in Palazzo Altemps, part of the National Roman Museum built in 1477 by Girolamo Riario.

94 top left The Triptych showing the Ascension, the Pentecost and the Final Judgement of the Blessed Angel is displayed in the Gallery of Ancient Art, in Palazzo Corsini. This is one of the finest works of Guido di Pietro Tosini, follower of the ideas of Brunelleschi and Masaccio.

94 bottom left The Hall of Perspectives in Palazzo Farnese is the work of Baldassarre Peruzzi (1481-1526). This buiilding, designed by Peruzzi himself in 1510 for the Siena banker Agostino Chigi, is possibly the most important work by the Tuscan artist. Sodoma, Raphael and a number of his followers also worked on the villa.

From the south-east corner of the square you can make your way along Via delle Quattro Fontane to Palazzo Barberini. This building, like so many others in the city, was embellished by very finest architects and artists of the period, among them Maderno, Bernini and Borromini. It now houses a museum and the Galleria Nazionale dell'Arte Antica. Highlights of its stunning collections include Raphael's celebrated *Fornarina* (a portrait of the woman reputed to be his lover), Caravaggio's *Narcissus*, Titian's *Venus and Adonis*, Lotto's *The Mystical Marriage of Saint Catherine* and a triptych by Beato Angelico. There are also works by Rubens, Van Dyck and Murillo.

94 top right La Fornarina *by Raphael, in the National Gallery of Ancient Art, is believed to have been the painter's lover.*

94 bottom right This painting displayed in Palazzo Corsini shows Henry VIII, and is the work of Hans Holbein the Younger. The works in the National Gallery of Ancient Art date from the 12th to the 18th centuries and come from various collections (di Torlonia, Barberini, Chigi, Sciarra, Hertz), purchased and donated.

95 top The Sarcophagus of the Spouses, in the Museum of Villa Giulia, is one of the most significant of its kind in Etruscan art. It dates back to 510 BC and was found in Cerveteri. It shows two figures (newly-weds at a banquet) modelled with great plastic mastery, in a classical Ionian style, with great clarity in the volumes and balance of form, typical of the Attic school.

95 bottom left The great Cista Ficoroni (so called from the name of the owner of the land in which it was discovered in the 18th century, in Palestrina), is in the Museum of Villa Giulia, and is a fine example of the refinement achieved by the Etruscans in the art of bronze. The body of the "cista" (a container used for manuscripts or women's toiletries) is embellished with an etching of the myth of the Argonauts. The name of the artist, Novios Plautios of Rome, is written on the handle.

95 bottom right The Chigi vase is in Hall 15 of the Etruscan Museum in Villa Giulia. This pottery amphora shows three separate scenes. In the top we see warriors heading off to battle, the middle shows the Caledonian boar hunt and the Judgement of Paris, and the lower section contains scenes of hare coursing with dogs. The vase comes from Formello (Veio) and is one of the most significant examples of late-proto-Corinthian art (640-625 BC).

In Rome's environs is another exceptional site: Villa Giulia and the Etruscan Museum. Its antiquities include the Warrior's Tomb (second half of the sixth century B.C.) complete with bronze helmet and shin-guards, the Husband and Wife Sarcophagus (530 B.C.) depicting a couple banqueting, the Chigi vase (a wine jug from Formello), one of the most significant examples of late proto-Corinthian ceramics, and the Ficoroni Cista (late fourth century B.C.), a coffer engraved with an episode from the saga of the Argonauts, unearthed in Palestrina in 1738. Villa Giulia is a classic example of Mannerist architecture. It was built for Pope Julius III (hence its name) to a design by Bartolomeo Ammanati and Vignola. Characterized by elegant views and exuberant décor, the villa has a two-storey façade featuring a large avant-corps that terminates with corner pillars.

This tour would not be complete without the Museo Borghese: Antonio Canova's statue of Pauline Bonaparte; Bernini's David, capturing the moment when he released the stone that killed Goliath (the sculptor allegedly modelled the face on his own); *Apollo and Daphne*, considered Bernini's finest statue; Caravaggio's *Madonna of the Serpent* (portraying the Madonna as she destroys a serpent with the aid of her Son, the painting expresses the "equo par condicio" between the Roman Catholic Church, insisting sin could be conquered only through the grace of the Virgin Mary, and the Protestant Church which believed Christ alone could forgive sins); Raphael's *Deposition*; Titian's *Sacred and Profane Love*.

96 left Apollo and Daphne, *by Bernini, displayed in the Galleria Borghese, is the youthful masterpiece of the artist born in Naples, but who moved to Rome when he was only seven. Pope Paul V Borghese, painted by the sculptor in 1618, expressed the desire that Bernini would become "the great Michelangelo of his century". This was effectively the case and this sculptor shows exactly why.*

97 bottom The David with Catapult *by Bernini is in the Galleria Borgese. The face is a self-portrait of the artist. Together with* Apollo and Daphne, Aeneas and Anchyses *and* the Rape of Prosperine, *this is one of a series of groups sculpted for the Borghese family by the great artist, famous for the design of the colonnade of St. Peter's, the altar and fountains, and palaces in Rome.*

96 bottom L'Amor Sacro e l'Amor Profano *(Sacred Love and Profane Love) is one of the most important works of Titian (Tiziano Vecellio), dated between 1515 and 1516. This painting represents the achievement of chromatic classicism by the artist from Pieve di Cadore. It is the last painting by Titian inspired by Giorgione. The two splendid figures of love seem involved in a silent but intense conversation.*

96-97 Paolina Borghese, a sculpture by Antonio Canova between 1805 and 1808, is displayed in the Galleria Borghese. Even though there is a certain contrast between the evocation of the triumphant Venus and the stiff drapes of the triclinium, this sculpture is one of the most successful works by the artist.

97 top The Deposition *by Raphael in Hall 9 of the Galleria Borghese was painted in 1507 for Atalanta Baglioni in memory of her son Grifonetto, and was hung in the church of St. Francis in Perugia. Even though this is considered one of the less successful works of the painter from Urbino,* the Deposition *does show the genius of Raphael, as we can see in the beautiful nude figure of Christ.*

98 top This aerial photograph shows the Quirinale, today the seat of the President. The building was begun in 1573 by Martino Longhi The Elder and continued from 1578 to 1585 by Ottaviano Mascherino. Built as the summer residence of the Popes, it was later extended by Fontana, Ponzio, Maderno and Bernini.

98-99 The Quirinale bears the name of the hill on which it was built. Before the current building, the summit of the hill was occupied by the 15th-century villa of Cardinal Oliviero Carafa, followed by the residence of Cardinal Ippolito d'Este. The façade is by Fontana and is conceived in accordance with the forms of the late Renaissance.

99 top left The Corazzieri *are the guards entrusted with the protection of the President, even though they are decorative rather than an effective force of protection. Only soldiers who pass strict selection procedures are able to enter this regiment.*

We left our previous itinerary in the vicinity of the Trevi Fountain. A short uphill walk along Via della Dataria brings you back to Palazzo del Quirinale. This grandiose building was erected on Rome's highest hill by pope Gregory XIII who used it as a summer residence to which he escaped from frequent malaria epidemics. Work on it started in 1574 but many artists were still adding finishing touches two centuries later: Bernini designed the façade overlooking Via del Quirinale, Domenico Fontana the main façade, and Carlo Maderno the chapel. After the unification of Italy it became the royal palace and, since 1947, the presidential palace.

99 top centre
The Yellow Room of the Quirinale, like nearly all the rooms, is covered with stuccoes and frescoes.

99 bottom centre
The photograph shows the First Reception Hall of the Quirinale. Among the works contained in the building are painting by Giulio Romano (St. John the Baptist), *Botticelli (The triptych with the Transfiguration, St.Gerolamo and St. Augustine) and Lorenzo Lotto, with the* Triumph of Chastity.

99 right
The Courtyard of Honour in the Quirinale is designed in the strict forms of the Counter-Reformation. The left wing was designed by Fontana, and the right by Ponzio. In the background is the 16th-century Palace of the Mascherino, with a five-arched double lodge and a crowned corner turret.

100 left
The reconstruction work on the Bath-house of Caracalla began in A.D. 212. The complex was completed by Heliogabalus and Alexander Severus and, after the restoration by Aurelian, remained in use until 537, when Vitis King of the Goths gave the command to cut the Antonian aqueduct, which had supplied the 80,000-litre tanks.

100 right The floor plan of the Bath-house of Caracalla follows the rules laid down in the 2nd century AD, with a great central body of 220 metres in length and 114 broad surrounded by enclosed green areas, in the form of a square of 330 metres per side. The entrance opened onto the Via Nova, parallel to the Appian Way.

100-101 In this aerial view we can see the Bath-House of Caracalla more clearly. This could hold 1,600 people and was the most famous bathing complex of imperial Rome. Even though only the walls remain, these are impressive in their size and give an idea of how the original structure must have appeared.

The Capitoline, Palatine and Quirinale hills are three landmarks in Rome's history. But the verdant Caelian, named after Caelius Vibenna, a hero of the wars against the Tarquins, has also played an important role. In the days of imperial Rome this was a fashionable residential district, and there are many archaeological remains here to prove it: the ruins of the Temple of Claudius; blocks of travertine stone built into the base of the bell-tower of the church of St. Giovanni and St. Paolo; the Arch of Dolabella (first century A.D.), one of the city's gates, later incorporated into the aqueduct Nero built to supply water to the Palatine; and, above all, the Baths of Caracalla, one of the most imposing structures of ancient Rome. Inaugurated by the emperor in A.D. 217, they had the capacity for over 1,600 bathers who came here to pursue their cultural and social interests as well as personal hygiene. The baths were, in effect, a multi-facility leisure centre. They remained in operation for three centuries until Goth invaders shut down the aqueduct that supplied the complex with water.

101 left Connected to the central body of the complex, occupied by the stadium, were secondary gymnasiums, schools for gymnasts and the Greek and Latin schools, with the steps resting against the water tanks. The central body was reached from four doors. Along the entrance axis were the frigidarium, the basilica in the centre covered by three cross-vaults, the tepidarium and the circular calidarium (with a diameter of 34 metres). In this picture, we can see the gardens.

101 top right During the 16th century excavations at the Bath-house of Caracalla, the Farnese Bull was found, a sculpture showing the myth of the martyrdom of Dyrces.

101 bottom right All the bath complexes were decorated with frescoes and mosaics.

102 top The mausoleum of Augustus is a circular building with a diameter of 87 metres, inspired by the tomb of Mausolos, king of Caria. It was begun by Augustus in 27 BC, for himself and his successors. In ancient times it lost its function as an imperial tomb, was transformed into a stone quarry, vineyard, hanging garden, amphitheatre, theatre and auditorium.

102 centre Here we see the temples of Vesta and Virile Fortune in Piazza della Bocca della Verità. The first has a circular plan and the second is rectangular.
The temple of Vesta - so called because the circular form made it resemble the place of worship of the Vestal Virgins - was built for Hercules the Victor.

103 left
This ancient marble wheel showing the enormous head of a triton with gaping mouth is better known as the Mouth of Truth. It is situated under the portico of Santa Maria in Cosmedin and is one of Rome's best known attractions. It is said that in medieval times it was used as a judge against liars, with no right of appeal. Those accused of lying had to place their hand inside the mouth and repeat what they had said.
If they were lying their hand was cut off.
It would appear, however, that the punishment was not so divine, and that there was a guard armed with a sharp sword concealed inside the monument, who cut off the hand of the unfortunate victim.

103 top right The temple of Virile Fortune was identified at the start of the twentieth century as the place of worship of the god Portunus, the protector of the nearby port on the river. It remains virtually intact, with the exception of a few alterations made in 872, when it was transformed into a Christian church.

102 bottom
The sacred area of Piazza Argentina is of great archaeological importance, as it is the largest visible complex from the Republican period. The zone is in the central part of the ancient Martial Field and was unearthed during the excavations from 1926 to 1929.

After making your way down from the Caelian, there is really only one direction to take: along Via del Circo Massimo across the Aventine. Don't forget to make a brief stop to admire the Bocca della Verità (Mouth of Truth): according to legend, this mascaron portraying a river god snaps shut on the hands of liars. You reach the Tiber at the point where it is crossed by the Ponte Sublicio. Right here is the Forum Boarium, the cattle market of ancient Rome. And on this site are the city's two best preserved temples. The rectangular one is known as the Temple of Fortuna Virilis (second to first centuries B.C.) and it was dedicated to Portunus, the god who protected the nearby river port. It has four columns at the front and half-columns set into the side and rear walls. In 872 this pagan temple was converted into the Christian church of Santa Maria Egiziaca. The other, circular building (second century B.C.) is known as the Temple of Vesta (on account of its resemblance to the one in the Forum) but scholars believe it was dedicated to Hercules. This ancient structure holds a record: it is the oldest building made of marble in existence. In 1100 this temple too became a place of worship for Christians, dedicated to Saint Steven. Nearby you can see what remains of the second largest amphitheatre of imperial Rome (the largest was built by Pompey). Work on the structure commenced under Julius Caesar and it was eventually dedicated by Augustus in memory of his nephew and son-in-law Marcellus. It must have been an imposing sight. The cavea, about 130 metres across, had a travertine façade embellished by three orders of columns (only a few Doric and Ionic ones have survived). Vestiges of the layout show that a series of ramps and ambulatories ensured the smooth flow of spectators entering and leaving the theatre. Abandoned in the fifth century, it was subsequently used as a quarry, fortress and, lastly, a patrician palace. Not far away in Largo Argentina (the old Campus Martius) is a further testimony to the grandeur of Rome outside the Imperial Fora. The Area Sacra is the largest group of temples from Republican times still visible in Rome. It was unearthed only in the late 1920s. There are remains of four temples from different periods, an altar erected by Postumius Albinus in memory of his grandfather, a consul, and at the rear of the circular temple, some tufa blocks believed to have been part of the Curia of Pompey where, on the Ides of March 44 B.C., Julius Caesar is said to have been assassinated. The very thought may send a shiver down your spine as you leave the Area Sacra and return to the river. The Tiber has always been considered a holy river and fount of life, sole remaining witness of the foundation of the settlement, and of its wars, passions and amazing achievements. The river (450 km long) has its source on Mount Fumaiolo in the Apennines, on the border between Tuscany and Emilia, and winds through the eternal city and flows on towards

103 bottom right The Theatre of Marcellus, of which only a few arches remain, is in the quarter of Sant'Angelo. The work was begun under Julius Caesar in 13 BC, and Augustus dedicated it to the memory of his nephew and son-in-law Marcellus.

This building too, which was abandoned in the 5th century, was used as a quarry for materials, a fortress and, finally, as a noble's palace.

104 top The statues of angels in Ponte Sant'Angelo were all designed by Bernini, but sculpted by his pupils. The angel with the robe and dice (left) is the work of Pietro Paolo Naldini, and the one with the cross (right) is by Ercole Ferrata.

104-105 Castel Sant'Angelo's gracious name is in contrast with the hard, essential architectural lines and the use that was made of it in the course of the centuries. From the 10th century onwards, this massive building became one of the strongholds of papal power. Cola di Rienzo took refuge within its imposing walls. Giordano Bruno, Cellini and Cagliostro were brought here by force and imprisoned in its terrible cells.

105 Along the bridge of Sant'Angelo are scenes showing the passion of Christ, summed up by the standing figures of angels. The angel with the sponge (above) is by Antonio Giorgetti, the angel with the crown of thorns (centre) is by Paolo Naldini and is a copy of an original sculpted by Gian Lorenzo Bernini, while the angel with the nails (below) was sculpted by Girolamo Lucenti.

the sea, first dividing into two branches (the Fiumara and Fiumicino) that form the so-called Isola Sacra. In the capital too the waters of this fascinating river briefly divide when they encounter a tiny patch of land. Tiber island was believed to have been built on harvested corn thrown into the Tiber by the Romans after Tarquinius Superbus was banished. Since ancient times it has been a centre of healing, sacred to Aesculapius. According to legend, a snake sacred to this deity was brought to Rome by Epidaurus to wipe out the plague of 293 B.C. When the creature saw the island, it slithered from the boat, reached its shores and made its home there. In remembrance of this episode, the Romans consacrated the island to the god of healing and shaped it like a boat. Standing in the river close to the island is a solitary arch, all that is left of the ancient "pons Aemilius" and now commonly known as the "Ponte Rotto" (broken bridge). It was rebuilt several times on account of the fast-flowing, eddying waters of the Tiber, even by Michelangelo, but to no avail. Two of its arches (besides the one still standing) were used in the construction of the adjacent Ponte Palatino. Another famous bridge across the Tiber is the Ponte Milvio, rebuilt along the Via Flaminia in 109 B.C. by the censor Marcus Emilius Scaurus, in the place of an older one. Constructed with blocks of tufa, it had four wide arches with lintels made of travertine. It acquired its present form in 1805 when restored by Giuseppe Valadier to mark the return

to Rome of Pius VII. Altogether more recent is the Ponte Vittorio Emanuele, forming the last stretch of Corso Vittorio Emanuele. Inaugurated to celebrate the fifitieth anniversary of the unification of Italy, the bridge has three arches supported by piers. It is decorated with four groups of statues carved from travertine, personifying Vanquished Oppression, United Italy, Allegiance to the Statutes and Liberty. At the very top of the columns are bronze sculptures of winged Victory.

106 top left When Hadrian built the bridge of Sant'Angelo to gain access to his tomb (A.D. 133-134), he named it Pons Aelius. With the change of role from tomb to fortress and papal residence, the bridge was rebuilt in accordance with the notions of beauty and power required by this new function. Under the artistic guidance of Gian Lorenzo Bernini, one of the finest examples of Roman Baroque was created, in the form of the ten statues of angels with the symbols of the Passion of Christ.

106 top right The bank of the Tiber in the Vatican ends with the Vittorio Emanuele II Bridge. Beyond this the avenue of the same name begins, one of the busiest streets in the city. The bridge was opened on the occasion of the celebrations for the 50th anniversary of the Kingdom of Italy, has three arches and is embellished with four sculpted groups in travertine stone.

106-107 In the course of its history, the island of Tiberina has had various names, including the Island of the Two Bridges, Licaonia and San Bartolomeo. However, this tongue of land formed by a bend in the Tiber in the centre of the city is one of the most memorable sights of the capital. The island played an important role in the urban settlement of the nearby hills, as it was a natural ford in the river.

107 top All that remains of the Aemilius Bridge today, solidly planted in the water, is one single arch. The rest of the bridge has been swept away by the currents of the Tiber and man. Today the Broken Bridge ("Ponte Rotto"), as it has been known for centuries, is there to bear witness to its ancient role. This crossing point over the Tiber was rebuilt on various occasions. The water at this point builds up such strong currents that the stability of the bridge is threatened over a long period. One of the contributors to the building work, with rather unsatisfactory results, was Michelangelo.

Nearby is Castel Sant'Angelo. It is reached across the bridge of the same name, first built by Hadrian to connect his mausoleum with the left bank of the Tiber and known in those days as "pons Aelius". Today the bridge is a stunning example of baroque, featuring ten statues of angels with symbols of Christ's Passion, created by Bernini. Just walking across it towards the ancient "Hadrianeum" can be an emotional experience in itself. The building has had many roles: commenced in A.D. 123 to serve as a mausoleum, it was later used as a fortress and eventually a prison. Cylindrical in shape and 64 metres in diameter, it was built in "opus caementicium", faced with tufa and travertine; it is surmounted by another smaller cylindrical structure. In the imperial period its exterior was embellished with statues. Still existing inside are three large rooms, one on top of another, that house the tombs, and a spiral ramp. As early as A.D. 271, under Aurelian, the mausoleum was converted into a fortress and encircled by imposing walls. Theodoric used it both as a citadel and as a prison. When Urban V, last of the Avignon popes, agreed to return to Rome he did so on one condition: that Castel Sant'Angelo be placed under papal dominion. He returned and the building was further fortified, with the addition of walls and towers. Today its huge bulk is contained within square walls with ramparts (named after the Sts. Matthew, Mark, Luke and John) at each corner. It houses the Museo Nazionale di Castel Sant'Angelo.

107 bottom The Ponte Milvio has very ancient origins, possibly dating back to the end of the 3rd century BC. Originally built of wood, it was demolished under the rule of the censor Marcus Emilius Scauro and rebuilt in stone. This structure has been altered on many occasions, and very little remains of the original Roman structure. The last significant renovation project dates back to 1805, and was the work of the architect Giuseppe Valadier, even though 50 years later Garibaldi's men partly blew it up to slow down the French advance. It was recovered in the second half of the 19th century by Francesco Azzurri.

108 top *The mosaics in the apse of Santa Maria in Trastevere, created after the death of Pope Innocent II, show Christ crowning the Virgin, a number of saints, including Innocent II and, at the level of the windows, the stories of the Virgin by Pietro Cavallini commissioned by Bertoldo Stefaneschi, whose portrait is in the central fresco.*

108-109 *The basilica of Santa Maria in Trastevere is in the square of the same name. This was decorated in the 17th century with a large octagonal tank by Carlo Fontana. According to tradition, the church was founded by St. Callistus, in the place where a "miraculous eruption of oil from the earth" occurred some years before the birth of Christ. This was probably crude petroleum. It was Julius (337 - 352) who ordered the construction of the basilica. The church we see today is the result of an elaborate building project under Innocent II between 1138 and 1148. The materials used are from the Bath-house of Caracalla.*

109 top Trastevere has always been considered the most genuine and popular quarter of Rome. The restaurants here are famous for their traditional specialities and reasonable prices.

109 centre The narrow tiled streets, the buildings in medieval style coloured with the washing hanging out to dry and a tranquil lifestyle make Trastevere resemble a small country town, even though it is actually one of the most popular destinations of international tourism.

109 bottom Trastevere is famous not only for its monuments and buildings, but for its people too. They say this is where the real Romans live, those with the lightning wit and cutting tongues. Trastevere, also known as the proletarian quarter of the city, exerts the same attraction as Saint-Germain in Paris and the Plaka in Athens.

Before full immersion in the awe-inspiring magnificence of the Vatican - just a short walk away - it is worth paying a visit to Trastevere, the only authentically working-class quarter of the historic city. Admittedly the old, low-priced trattorias that lined the narrow medieval streets and the ordinary, affable folk who populated Rome's "most Roman" quarter are fast disappearing, and their place is being taken by elegant restaurants, jazz clubs and trendy shops. But the quarter still has its own picturesque charm. Amid this maze of streets and alleys there are also some places of exceptional artistic interest. Most notably, the basilica of St. Maria in Trastevere, probably the first Christian church in Rome. It is traditionally believed to have been founded by pope Callixtus I in A.D. 217 on the site where a fountain of oil (probably petroleum) had miraculously sprung up from the ground in the year 38 B.C., an event later interpreted by Christians as an announcement of the coming of the Messiah. The basilica, which acquired its present plan in A.D. 337 under Julius I, has undergone many changes through the centuries but today's church is largely the structure erected between 1138 and 1148 by pope Innocent II. The stones used to build it were taken from the Baths of Caracalla.

PRINCIPIS APOST PAVLVS V BVRGHESIVS ROMANVS
ALEXAN VII P M

110 top left *This photograph shows the crowds that flock to St. Peter's for the Papal Angelus. At the centre of the square is the Vatican Obelisk. Caligula brought this from Egypt in the year 37 to adorn the Circus of Nero, where St. Peter was martyred.*

110 top right *The most important religious ceremonies take place in St. Peter's and its square, measuring 240 metres broad and 196 long at the widest part.*

110-111 *This is one of the most famous pictures in the world: the basilica of St. Peter's with the colonnade of Bernini and Michelangelo's dome.*

111 top *The Swiss Guards have been the armed corps of the Vatican for nearly 500 years. To enrol, a soldier has to be aged between 19 and 30, Catholic, unmarried and clean-shaven. The corps of guards is made up of 100 men, commanded by a colonel. Their task is to protect the Pope, with weapons if necessary.*

It is only a short step from Rome's first church to the greatest symbol in Christendom. Following the river as it winds past the Gianicolo (another of Rome's hills), you reach the massive Basilica of St.Peter's and the tiny state of the Vatican. From this city-state, last temporal home of the papacy, the popes have dictated the destiny of Rome and the entire Catholic world. The quantity of artworks and history preserved within this tiny area is mind-boggling. It is hardly surprising that seemingly endless queues are now part and parcel of the Vatican landscape, as visitors wait their turn to enter the basilica, ascend to the dome, tour the building that houses the Vatican Museums and gaze in wonder at the Sistine Chapel. You get a first insight into the splendours in store when standing in the magnificent square in front of St.Peter's, with the basilica's majestic dome rising above you. Designed by Gian Lorenzo Bernini, the oval-shaped piazza - 240 metres in width - comprises two hemicycles with a four-row colonnade converging at the two centre points of the oval. Embellishing the columns are 140 statues of saints and the coat of arms of Alexander VII, the pope who commissioned this grandiose project. At the centre of the square, supported by four bronze lions, is an obelisk that adorned the Forum Iulii in Alexandria; it was brought to Rome by Caligula in A.D. 37 and set in the circus later named after Nero. Pope Sixtus V decided to have it moved from its position at the side of the square to the centre, where it remained. In the Middle Ages it was called the *Aguglia* (the Needle) and the top section was believed to hold a bronze casket with Caesar's ashes: it actually contains a piece of wood from the cross. The basilica dedicated to Saint Peter was constructed in A.D. 320 on what was thought to be the site of the martyrdom (circa A.D. 64) of Christ's apostle, the first pope. Concealed beneath the massive edifice is a necropolis supposedly containing the tomb of Simon-renamed-Peter, chosen by Jesus to guide the Christian faith. That piece of land had previously been used to bury people considered as "damned". A small shrine stood over Peter's tomb. The first real church on the site was consecrated by pope Silvester I in 326. On either side of the nave were two aisles, flanked by rows of columns; in front of the main body of the building was a four-sided portico with holy water stoups in the middle. The church retained this structure for over 1,000 years. Then, in 1452, pope Nicholas V took the advice offered by Leon Battisti Alberti and decided to enlarge the apse. The project was entrusted to Bernardo Rossellino but, on the death of Nicholas V, work came to a standstill for over half a century and was only briefly resumed under Paul II. It was not until the papacy of Julius II that restructuring got under way. Bramante was called in as chief architect: showing total disregard for the building's history and works of art, he demolished more than half of the existing structure.

111 bottom St. Peter in the Chair *is a bronze by Arnolfo di Cambio (1245 ? - 1302), in the basilica of St. Peter's. It was believed for a long time that this work was from the 5th century, then a careful analysis led to the correct date and artist. An interesting curiosity: the right foot of the apostle is worn away because it has been touched by thousands of the faithful over the centuries as a sign of devotion.*

112 top left This photograph shows the Papal symbol in the Vatican gardens.

112 top right This view from the dome of St. Peter's shows the huge square and Via della Conciliazione. This broad street was built between 1936 and 1950, by literally emptying two historic quarters, Santo Spirito and Sant'Angelo.

The Greek-cross plan envisioned by the architect and pope died with them. The next superintendent of the new construction was the young Raphael - working in collaboration with Fra' Giocondo and Giuliano da Sangallo - who instead favoured a Latin-cross plan for the basilica. After Raphael, Michelangelo took over responsibility for the project and the plan of the basilica was changed yet again. Upon the artist's death other chief architects, including Giacomo della Porta and Domenico Fontana, were appointed and the work continued. For liturgical reasons and to cover the area occupied by the first basilica, Raphael's Latin-cross project was adopted once again: Carlo Maderno added three chapels on either side, bringing the nave and aisles forward to the present façade, which he completed in 1614 (even if the inscription says 1612). The basilica was consecrated by pope Urban VIII on November 18, 1626, 1,300 years after the dedication of the first church on this site. It is a building of unequalled size: with a floor area of over 22,000 square metres, it is 186 metres in length (including the thickness of its walls, 194 metres, and with the portico, 219 metres); its façade is 115 metres in width and 47 metres in height; its cupola has a diameter of 42.5 metres and a height of 137 metres. The supreme monument to Christianity was at last complete: the power of Catholicism and the papacy prevailed over the authority of all the earth's sovereigns, who here had to kneel in deference. Aptly inscribed on a stone in St.Peter's Square are the words: "Christus vincit, Christus regnat, Christus imperat".

112-113
This religious service was photographed inside St. Peter's. When particularly important ceremonies take place, such as the opening of the Jubilee or beatifications, the Pope faces out onto the great balustrade at the front of the church.

113 top The dome of St. Peter's is the work of Michelangelo, who was in charge of the work up to his death. The immense structure rests on a base of 16 buttresses formed by Corinthian columns. The crown, divided into 16 segments, has a double shell. It is possible to visit the dome by way of an outside entrance in the right side of the basilica.

113 bottom Some other prelates, accompanied by a large crowd of faithful and the ever-present Swiss Guards with their multicoloured uniform, take part in a religious ceremony.

You get a clear idea of the Church's predominance when you climb to the summit of the dome, follow narrow passageways and winding staircases up to the lantern. Inside the basilica the power of the Church is conveyed by outstanding works of art: for instance, the five doors created by artists from different periods (Filarete, Giacomo Manzù, Luciano Minguzzi); Michelangelo's *Pietà*, attacked by a madman determined to destroy symbols of idol worship; the bronze statue of St.Peter attributed to Arnolfo di Cambio (thirteenth century) but probably even older; Bernini's great bronze and gold canopy (29 metres high), standing over St.Peter's tomb; and the museum of papal treasures.

114 The Creation of Adam is one of the most famous of Michelangelo's frescoes. It is part of the series of painted stories on the ceiling of the Sistine Chapel. The artist finished his work on the ceiling after four years of continuous work.

But there is much more to the artistic heritage of the Church than the basilicas of St.Peter and St.John. Albeit small, the Vatican City contains enough masterpieces to turn any museum green with envy. In some ways the Vatican has replaced the Forum of ancient Rome. The splendours left by the emperors were destroyed by time, neglect and persecution of whatever was considered incompatible with Christianity. But they now live again in the splendours of the popes who, as patrons of art for two thousand years, created and gathered together countless extraordinary works of art. These collections are housed in the Vatican Museums, in buildings once occupied by Sixtus IV, Innocent VIII and Julius II and later extensions. Undisputed crowning glories of the works displayed are the Sistine Chapel, with ceiling panels painted by Michelangelo, and the Raphael Rooms, the private apartment of Julius II, decorated with

115-118 In the vast vault of the Sistine Chapel, Michelangelo decided to paint the history of humanity before the arrival of Christ. In this way, he connected up with the stories painted on the walls, which tell the life of Jesus Christ. The single figures on the ceiling are contained within a monumental painted architectural structure, laid over the true ceiling.

119 The original sin and the banishment of Adam and Eve from the Earthly Paradise are among the frescoes on the ceiling of the Sistine Chapel.

frescoes it took the artist and his pupils sixteen years to complete. In the Sistine Chapel the cardinals meet to elect the pope and other ceremonial functions are held. Commissioned by pope Sixtus IV and built by Giovannino de' Dolci (1475-1481), the chapel is entirely frescoed. The best time to see it is in the morning, when light streaming through the six large windows offers the perfect illumination for the masterpieces created by Michelangelo and the outstanding painters who contributed to this sublime testimonial to Renaissance art. It took Michelangelo four years to complete the ceiling (approximately 800 square metres). On the altar wall is his huge fresco of the Last Judgment, with figures large and small, architectural elements, symbolic imagery, their impact heightened by an amazing range of colours. After a ten-year restoration project the painting is once again revealed in all its original splendour.

120-121 Perugino's Handover of the Keys *is part of the cycle of frescoes in the Sistine Chapel. The decoration of the walls, to which this fresco belongs, tells the stories of Moses and Christ, and was painted by a team of artists including Botticelli, Domenico Ghirlandaio and Cosimo Rosselli, as well as Perugino.*

ZACHERIAS
ELEAZAR
MATHAN
IACOB
IOSEPH

IMENSV SALAMO
TEMPLVM TV
HOC QVARTE
SACRASTI

SIX TE OPIBVS
DISPAR
RELIGIONE
PRIOR

122 left This frescoed vault in the Raphael Rooms, in the Vatican Museums, was not painted by the artist, but by his pupils. Even though it was Julius II who commissioned Raphael to carry out the decoration of the papal apartments, the idea of embellishing these rooms had originally been that of Pope Nicholas.

122 top right The Dispute of the Sacrament *in the room of the Signatory is perhaps the most sublime work of Raphael. This room was almost entirely frescoed by Raphael between 1509 and 1511, and mixes the humanist culture linked to the classical tradition with the new research in perspectives.*

123 top left The battle of Ostia and the fire of Borgo are the subjects of the frescoes in the Room of the Fire, completed under Pope Leo X. The frescoes were produced by the disciples of Raphael by following his sketches, which dealt exclusively with episodes from the lives of Popes named Leo. The fire of Borgo, in the photograph, was put out by Leo IV by simply making the sign of the cross.

123 top right The fresco tells the story of the banishment of Heliodorus from the temple. The work was painted by Raphael between 1512 and 1514, assisted by Giulio Romano and Giovanni da Udine. The symbols, whose purpose is the exaltation of the Church, would appear to have been designed by Julius II.

122 centre right The School of Athens *was painted by Raphael between 1508 and 1511.*

122 bottom right Raphael's The Creation of the Animals, *in the lodge, is a fresco painted between 1515 and 1518. Begun by Bramante, it was completed by the young painter and his pupils, including Giovanni da Udine, Giulio Romano, Polidoro da Caravaggio and Perin Del Vaga. A total of 13 bays were decorated, 12 with scenes from the Old Testament and one with episodes from the New Testament.*

122-123 The Hall of Constantine is one of the rooms in the Vatican frescoed by Raphael. The painter from Urbino was in charge of the decoration from 1509 to 1517. The work was commissioned by Pope Julius II who, upon learning of the talents of the painter, sacked the artists who had previously been contracted (Perugino, Sodoma, Peruzzi, Lotto and Bramantino) to take on Raphael as sole artist. The Hall of Constantine was completed by Giulio Romano, Raffaelino and Giovanni Francesco Penni on the basis of the drawings left behind by the master.

124 left In the Pius-Clementine Museum, in the first alcove to the left of the Octagonal Courtyard (the work of Bramante), is the Apollo of Belvedere. *This extraordinary work is a copy of a sculpture - possibly in bronze - from the 4th century, attributed to Leocares and discovered at the end of the 15th century near San Pietro in Vincoli. The god was probably holding a bow and laurel branch bound in bandages, the symbol of his healing powers.*

124 top right Caravaggio's The Deposition *(1602 - 1604) is an oil on linen measuring three metres by two, kept in the Pinacoteca Vaticana. This collection of extraordinary paintings, with works by Raphael, Leonardo da Vinci, Beato Angelico and many other famous artists, was opened in 1816 by Pius VI, after Antonio Canova had recovered and brought to Rome 77 works which had become the property of the French after the Treaty of Tolentino.*

124 bottom right The Madonna of Foligno, *an important work kept in the Pinacoteca Vaticana, was painted by Raphael between 1512 and 1513, as an ex-voto of Sigismondo Conti, man of letters of Foligno and household secretary of Julius II. In the background, we can see a panoramic view of the Umbrian town. The painting has been housed in a number of locations, from the church of Aracoeli to the convent of Sant'Anna in Foligno and Paris. It was taken to Rome in 1816.*

125 The La *kept in the P Clementine is a copy of a original, sc Greek marb Agesandros sons Polydo Athenodoros in the 1st century. The sculpted group was found in the Domus Aurea in 1506.*

The Vatican Museums form a vast complex and it would take a lifetime to see every single item of their collections. Amid this abundance of paintings, sculptures, jewels, statuary, and sacred vestments, there is even a good Egyptian Museum.

It is pointless to try to cram too much into a single visit. And after walking down miles of corridors, through halls, across rooms, the stamina of even the most determined visitor starts to wane - as is evident from the museums' three first-aid posts and the café where the faint and weary can recharge their batteries. To prevent visitors from losing their way in the labyrinthine complex, four colour-coded itineraries have been devised, to be selected according to areas of interest or time available. All four itineraries start from the Circular Gallery, reached from the imposing spiral ramp that goes up to the ticket offices. In summer visitors enter the museums through the Cortile delle Corazze, now home of the Antonine Column, erected in A.D. 161 as a tribute to emperor Antoninus Pius.

Among the many exceptional exhibits in the Pio-Clementine Museum are the *Apoxyomenos*, a copy of a bronze statue by Lysippus depicting the athlete as he wipes his body with a strigil, the *Laocoon* by Agesandros and the *Apollo of Belvedere*, attributed to Leochares. Preserved in the Pinacoteca Vaticana, founded by Pope Pius VI, are Giotti's *Stefaneschi Triptych*; the *Transfiguration*, started by Raphael and completed after his death by Giulio Romano; the *Madonna di Foligno*, also by Raphael, commissioned as a votive offering by Sigismondo Conti, a man of letters from Foligno; Leonardo da Vinci's *St. Jerome* and Caravaggio's *Deposition*.

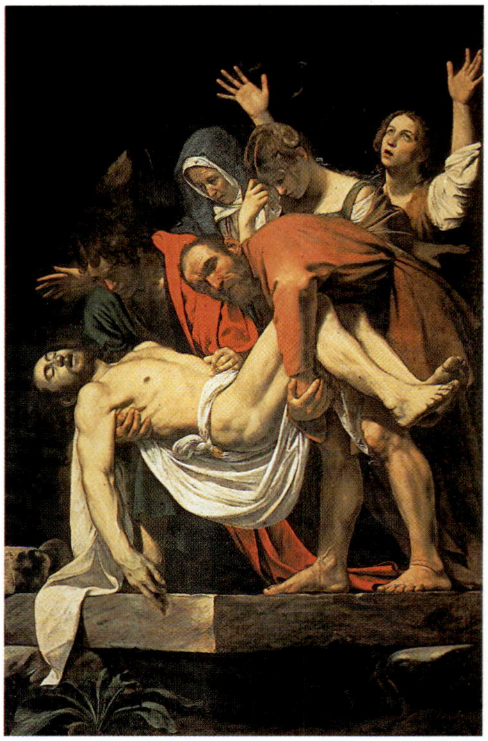

126 top The aerial photo covers the garden and palaces housing the Vatican Museums. Vatican City is an independent state occupying 0.44 square kilometres. As well as all the territory within the Vatican walls, the microscopic country also includes the Lateran Buildings, the Cancelleria, the Propaganda Fide, the hospital of Bambin Gesù and Castel Gandolfo. The state has 550 inhabitants, mints its own coins, has a radio and television station, its own newspaper and its own police force (the Swiss Guards).

126-127 The triptych Stefaneschi by Giotto is one of the most important works on display in the Pinacoteca Vaticana. The triptych takes its name from Cardinal Jacopo Stefaneschi, who commissioned it for the great altar of St. Peter's.

126 bottom left The Apostolic Library of the Vatican is part of the Vatican Museums. Founded by Sistus IV in 1475, it was enriched in the course of the centuries with manuscripts and printed texts of great value. There is a total of 75,000 volumes in manuscript, 70,000 archives, 100,000 original handwritten texts and around 80,000 printed books.

In the Vatican Library is the celebrated *Aldobrandini Wedding*, one of the rarest frescoes to survive since antiquity, re-discovered in 1605 near the Arch of Gallieno, on the Esquiline. There could be no more eloquent testimony to the magnificence of these treasures than the practically permanent queue of visitors who wait patiently outside the Vatican walls for their turn to enter this shrine of art. Ancient Egyptian, Greek, Etruscan, Early Christian, Renaissance and modern art: the entire artistic history of mankind is represented in the Museums' seemingly interminable rooms. This legacy, formed over the course of millennia, traces its almost chance origins to a furrow ploughed on the nearby Palatine Hill 2,700 years ago.

126 bottom right The Map Gallery, 120 metres long, takes its name from the maps of Italy frescoed on the walls between 1580 and 1583 by Antonio Danti, on the instructions of his brother, the Dominican friar Egnazio Danti, mathematician, architect and cosmographer.

127 bottom
The Aldobrandini Wedding *is a splendid fresco from the Augustan period, kept in the hall of the same name adjacent to the Apostolic Library of the Vatican. It shows the preparations for the marriage of Alexander the Great and Roxanne. It was rediscovered in 1605 near the arch of Gallienus.*

128 top Santa Maria Maggiore, whose façade we see here, is known as the Liberian or Santa Maria ad Neves, because it was built, according to a legend, by Pope Liberius on the site of a miraculous snowstorm. This place of worship, like many others in Rome, has undergone many alterations in the course of the centuries.

128-129 The photograph shows the inside of the basilica of San Giovanni in Laterano. This is the cathedral of Rome. Dedicated to St. Saviour, St. John the Baptist and St. John the Evangelist, the Constantinian basilica was built between 313 and 318, and had a similar layout to that of the ancient St. Peter's. From that time, it was restored on many occasions. With Sistus V, the Lodge of the Blessings was added, under Clement VIII the transept was decorated and Francesco Borromini remodelled the naves under Innocent X. The imposing, severe façade dates from the 18th century, and was designed by Alessandro Galilei.

129 left The cloister of the basilica of San Giovanni in Laterano is a masterpiece of "Cosmatesque" art. It was built between 1215 and 1232 by Vasalleto (as we can see from an inscription on the frieze of the portico). Small arches rest on columns of various shapes. Along the walls of the cloister, we can admire sculptures, burial slabs and materials from Roman and early Christian excavations, all found inside the ancient church.

No other religious building in Rome more effectively expresses the greatness of the papacy and its authority (as was, moreover, its architects' intentions). But another basilica used by the popes - St. Giovanni in Laterano - has a no less stirring effect on visitor's emotions. It is the cathedral church of Rome and second-most important place of worship in the city. Its basic structure reflects the layout of the original St.Peter's, with twin aisles on either side of the nave. Its façade, lavishly adorned with statues, was re-designed by Alessandro Galilei in the eighteenth century. Before the papacy moved to Avignon in 1309, the adjoining Lateran Palace was the official residence of the popes, who were crowned in the basilica until 1870. The palace contains the Holy Staircase and the Sancta Sanctorum, the chapel of St.Lawrence built by Nicholas III in 1278. Today the church is the titular see of the pope as bishop of Rome and the pontiff celebrates Maundy Thursday services here.

129 top right This fresco by Masolino da Panicale (1383-1440) - St. Catherine and the idolater empress - is in the chapel of St. Catherine, in the left nave of the upper basilica of St. Clement. On the avenue of San Giovanni in Laterano, this splendid building, which also includes a convent and a lower basilica, was built on a the site of a 2nd-century house. The building was damaged by the Normans, was rebuilt by Pasquale II following the pattern of the ancient religious complex. The layout of the church and the bell tower date from 1713-1719.

129 bottom right The Triumph of the Cross is in the basin of the apse in the upper basilica of St. Clement. From the Roman School, this dates from the first half of the 12th century. At the centre of the mosaic we can see the crucifix with the Virgin and St. John at the sides.

130 top left St. Paul outside the Walls is the biggest basilica in Rome after St. Peter's. It was built where the saint was buried, according to tradition. It was consecrated by Sylvester I in 324, rebuilt by Valentinian II, Theodosus and Arcadius, reconsecrated by Pope Siricius in 390 and completed in its current dimensions by Honorius in 395, In July 1823 the church was almost completely destroyed by fire, and was rebuilt following the original design and reconsecrated in 1854 by Pius IX.

130 bottom left The photograph shows the inside of the church of Santo Stefano Rotondo, the oldest circular church in Rome, dated around the 5th century. In the 12th century a portico was added and the outer circular colonnade was eliminated in the 15th century.

130 top right The mosaic of the triumphal arch of the basilica of San Prassede shows Christ blessing with, from the left the Sts. Paul, Praxedes and Pasquale I, who is offering the church, to the right the Sts. Peter, Prudence and Zeno. The origins of the basilica are linked to the "titulus Praxedis", or Praxedes, the daughter of the senator Prudent and sister of Prudence. In 489 there was already a place of worship on the site, but it was Pope Pasquale I who gave the impulse for the building of the imposing basilica. The Pope removed the bodies of 2,000 martyrs from the catacombs and moved them here.

130 bottom right The dome of Sant'Andrea della Valle is the highest in Rome after the cupola of St. Peter's. The frescoes of the cupola and apse are among the finest examples of Roman Baroque. The church was built in the first half of the 17th century, from a design by Carlo Maderno.

131 left The Moses *of Michelangelo in San Pietro in Vincoli is a severe and imposing statue. This is one of the many sculptures that formed part of the monumental tomb of Pope Julius II. Michelangelo had signed the contract for the execution of the work in 1513, but the sudden death of the Pope led to the stoppage of work. This was restarted in 1516, and the funerary monument was completed in 1545, but was much smaller and different in layout from the original design.*

131 top right The dome of the church of San Carlino alle Quattro Fontane was designed by Francesco Borromini. The decoration of the dome is incredible, with concentric circles forming crosses, octagons and hexagons, reminiscent of the patterns formed by the beads of a rosary.

131 bottom right The ecstasy of St. Theresa, or St. Theresa Transfixed by the Love of God *(1646), is one of the masterpieces of Gian Lorenzo Bernini. It is situated on the alter of the Cappella Cornaro, in the church of Santa Maria della Vittoria. The statues of the Cornaro family were also sculpted by Bernini and his pupils.*

136 Nicknamed "er cupolone" by the Romans on account of its enormous size, the dome of St. Peter's is a very visible sign of the temporal power of the Church. Designed by Michelangelo who supervised the work until his death, it comprises a double calotte erected on a base supported by 16 huge buttresses that project from coupled Corinthian columns.

Between the columns are large tympanum-style windows. The dome has an external circumference of 58 metres and is 50.35 metres high.

INDEX

Page numbers followed by "c" refer to captions

PHOTO CREDITS

Marcello Bertinetti / Archivio White Star: Pages 1, 8-9, 12 bottom, 57 top, 66 bottom, 71 bottom, 74 top left, 81 top, 83, top, 84-85, 85 centre left, 87 top, 88 top, 104 top, 105, 109, 110 top, 111 top, 112 top left, 112-113, 113 top, 126 centre and bottom, 128 top.

Marcello Bertinetti / Archivio White Star "Concessione S.M.A. N° 316 dal 18.08.1995": Pages 11 top, 71 centre, 72-73, 73 bottom, 82 top, 86 top left, 88 centre and bottom, 98 top, 102 top.

Marcello Bertinetti / Archivio White Star "Concessione S.M.A. N° 325 dal 01.09.1995": Pages 14-15, 16-17, 58, 60-61, 64, 65, 74-75, 76-77, 77 bottom 78 bottom left, 80, 100-101, 104-105, 106 top left, 106-107, 112 top right.

AFE Foto: Pages 53 centre, 54 top left.

Giulio Veggi / Archivio White Star: Pages 9 top, 12 top, 59 left, 59 centre and bottom right, 62 top, 62-63, 63, 64-65, 65 top right, 70-71, 72, 73 top, 78 top, 79 top left, 82 bottom, 82-83, 100, 101, 102 bottom, 103, 107, 128-129.

AKG Photo: Pages 25 bottom, 26 bottom, 28 centre, 29 bottom, 31 top, 32-33, 33 bottom, 35 top, 40-41, 40 bottom, 41 centre, 43 top, 46 top and bottom, 47 bottom, 49 centre and bottom, 96 bottom, 122 right, 124 top right.

Stefano Amantini / Atlantide: Pages 57 bottom, 108-109.

Massimo Borchi / Atlantide: Pages 98-99, 99 right.

Fabrizio Borra - Focus Team: Pages 70 top, 71 top, 78 top left.

Giovanni Dagli Orti: Pages 20 top, 22 bottom, 23 centre, 25 top right, 28-29, 31 bottom left, 33 top, 34 bottom, 35 bottom, 38, 38-39, 39 bottom, 41 bottom, 46-47, 47 top, 50 centre and bottom, 56 bottom, 89 top right, 93 top and bottom right, 96-97, 97 bottom, 126-127, 129 centre.

Giancarlo Costa / Ag. Stradella: Pages 28 bottom, 34 top left, 44 top, 45 bottom, 50, top 50-51.

Araldo De Luca: Pages 8 bottom, 13, 19, 20 bottom, 68 top, 67 top left, 92 bottom, 93 bottom left, 95 top, 95 bottom, 96 top, 125, 131 left.

E.T. Archive: Pages 27 bottom, 31 bottom right, 32 top, 34-35, 48 left.

Farabola Foto: Pages: 52-53, 53 top, 54 bottom, 56 centre.
Fototeca Storica Nazionale: Pages 41 top, 42 top, 43 bottom, 44 bottom, 45 right, 52 top, 53 bottom.

Cesare Gerolimetto: Pages 8 top, 59 top right, 74 top right, 85 top, 85 centre right, 85 bottom, 86-87, 87 bottom, 90-91, 91, 99 top left, 102 centre, 106 top right, 130 left, 130 bottom right, 136.

Johanna Huber / SIME: Page 129 top.

Andrea Iemolo: Page 79 top right

Mary Evans Picture Library: Pages 21 right, 30-31, 36 centre, 36 bottom left, 36-37, 37 top.

Nippon Television Corporation: Pages 114, 115-118, 119.

Luciano Pedicini / Archivio Dell'Arte: Pages 92-93, 95 centre.

Archivio Scala: Pages 21 left, 22-23 top, 23 top, 22-23 bottom, 24-25, 25 top left, 26-27, 28 top, 30 top, 30-31 top, 34 top right, 35 centre, 36 top, 36 bottom left, 39 top, 42 bottom, 42-43, 44-45, 48-49, 49 top, 51 top, 68 bottom, 68-69, 67 left, 67 bottom right, 75, 76, 89 top left, 92 top, 94, 97 top, 108 top, 111 bottom, 120-121, 122 left, 122-123, 123 top, 124 left, 124 bottom left, 127 bottom, 129 bottom, 130 top right, 131 right.

Lorenzo Sechi / SIE: Page 113 bottom.

Giovanni Simeone / SIME: Pages 3-6, 10-11, 56-57, 66 top, 80-81, 86 top right, 88-89, 90, 110-111, 126 top, 129 top.

The Kobal Collection: 54 top, 55 top, 55 bottom.

MUSEUM AND ART COLLECTIONS

Alte Pinakothek - Munich: Page 42-43.
Archaeological Museum - Ostia: Page 25 top right.
Archaeological Museum- Venice: Page 28 top.
Belgian Royal Library - Bruxelles: Page 41 top.
Biblioteca Vaticana - Rome: Page 41 centre.
Bonnat - Bayonne: Page 48 top left.
Ca' Rezzonico - Venice: Page 25 bottom.
Canova Museum- Possagno: Pages 48 bottom left.
Capitoline Museum - Rome: Pages 20, 22 bottom, 23 centre, 31 bottom left, 33 top, 34 bottom, 36 bottom, 39 bottom, 68 bottom, 68-69, 67.
Document Jean Vinchon - Paris: Page 41 bottom.
Galleria Borghese - Rome: Pages 22-23 bottom, 96, 97.
Galleria D'Arte Moderna - Florence: Page 51 top.
Galleria degli Uffizi - Florence: Page 23 top.
Galleria Doria Pamphilj - Rome: Page 75.
Galleria Nazionale d'Arte Antica - Rome: Pages 94 right, 94 top left.
Historical Museum - Bucarest: Pages 35 bottom, 46-47.
Kunsthistorisches Museum - Wien: Page 40 bottom.
Louvre Museum - Paris: Pages 22-23 top, 38-39.
Musée d'Orsay, Paris: Page 33 bottom.
Musée de l'Armée - Parigi: Page 50 centre right.
Museo del Risorgimento - Turin: Page 50 bottom.
Museo delle Terme - Rome: Pages 35 centre, 92 top, 93 top and bottom right.
Museum Narodowe - Krakau: Pages 32-33.
National Gallery of Art - Washington: Page 49 bottom.
Niedersäschisisches Landesmuseum - Hannover: Page 49 centre.
Oratorio di S. Silvestro - Rome: Pages 40-41.
Palace of Versailles: Page 47 top.
Palatine Antiquarium - Rome: Page 76
Palazzo Ducale - Mantua: Page 36 top.
Palazzo Madama - Rome: Pages 24-25.
Palazzo Pitti - Florence: Page 50 centre left.
Pinacoteca Vaticana - Rome: Pages 124 right, 126-127, 127 bottom.
Pio-Clementine Museum - Vatican City: Pages 8 bottom, 21 left, 39 top, 124 left, 125.
Puskin Museum- Mosca: Page 24 bottom.
Quartiere delle guardie Nobili - Vatican: Pages 48-49, 49 top.
Raphael Rooms - Vatican: Pages 42 bottom, 122, 123.
St. Peter - Vatican City: Page 13
Vatican Museums - Braccio Nuovo - Roma: Pages 34 top right.

Map by Monica Falcone